# Moving
## Beyond
### Broke

# Moving
# Beyond
# Broke

## THE POWER OF
## PERSEVERANCE IN
## PERSONAL FINANCE

## DASHA KENNEDY

**Simon Acumen**

New York   Amsterdam/Antwerp   London   Toronto   Sydney   New Delhi

SIMON
ACUMEN

*To my mother, Shirese, and my late father, John,*
*Thank you for sacrificing everything you wanted to*
*give me everything I needed.*

*To my sons, Camryn and Woo, just as my parents*
*sacrificed their dreams to make mine possible,*
*I have poured my heart into paving the way for yours.*

*This one is for y'all.*

# Contents

# Moving Beyond Broke

# *Reality Check*

I still remember the sound of the calculator echoing in my empty apartment. Clicking and clacking. The sound of the buttons filled the silence in the room, and each one was a reminder of the financial hole I had dug myself into. I sat there punching numbers, trying to make sense of a budget that never seemed to balance, credit card debt that never seemed to decrease, and bill collectors who never seemed to stop calling.

**I just had to accept it for what it was. I was broke.**

Chances are, if you've picked up this book, maybe you've found yourself in a similar spot. Or you may be familiar with my story, or maybe the name The Broke Black Girl caught your attention. But the truth is, I didn't always know how to move beyond being broke, and society wasn't helping.

There is an unfair stigma that surrounds the idea of "being broke." Being broke is often associated with the reputation of irresponsibility, laziness, or lack of ambition. These misconceptions cast a heavy cloud of shame, silence, and self-doubt on those facing financial hardships and treat "being broke" as a permanent destination instead of a starting point or brief stop on someone's journey. **No one** *chooses* **to be broke.** While it's true that our personal finance decisions play a major role in our financial status, the underlying factors around money reveal a different story that extends beyond personal choices. It's a journey I am all too familiar with, and that's why I wrote this book. *Moving Beyond Broke* is not just another financial guide—it's a testament to the resilience and strength required to transform your financial life.

Financial insecurity isn't just a matter of numbers not adding up on the back of an envelope or in an Excel spreadsheet; it's an issue that affects all aspects of our lives. Where we live, where we work, what we eat, whom we date—all the way down to the size of our family. It influences our mental health, our professional and personal relationships, and our overall well-being. If you've ever tried to have a good time while worrying about bills, debt, or any expected or unexpected expenses, you know firsthand how financial stress can overshadow even the happiest moments. Yet despite this experience being so common among us, conversations about personal finance often leave out the most important element: the human experience.

I get it. I grew up in a family who did not discuss money. Raised by teenage parents who were not of age to work traditional nine-to-five jobs or even be legally employable, I became aware of the weight of financial challenges at a very young age. By the time I reached my teenage years, I had already developed several unhealthy financial perspectives that would follow me into adulthood. I viewed money as a source of stress and uncertainty rather than a tool for empowerment and security. I avoided discussing anything money-related because I had never witnessed open and constructive conversations about finances in my family.

It wasn't until I was nineteen, while working at a Fortune 500 financial institution, that I realized just how clueless I was about money.

The way my coworkers talked about money felt like they were speaking a different language. I mean, they exuded money, from the clothes they wore to the cars they drove and their overall demeanor. As someone coming out of high school right into corporate America, these markers of success seemed like the ultimate goal to me. For the first time in my life, I was hearing people use phrases like "401(k)," "investment portfolio," "retirement," and "emergency savings account." It was clear that they had reached a level of financial literacy that I could not even grasp. These conversations were being led by people twice my age, triple my net worth, individuals who did not look like me and spoke about money in ways that felt disconnected from my reality. I knew that there had to be a simpler way for everyday people like me, wanting to move beyond being broke, to understand and improve our financial situation while also validating my experience as a Black woman.

Have you ever felt that way? Listening to other people talk about money like it's second nature while you are left sitting there like an outsider? That feeling of shame and guilt weighing on your chest for not being able to add *something* to the conversation. Then it's not just the terminology that is confusing, it's the overwhelming feeling that you don't belong in the conversation at all. Why do we feel this way? Why does it seem like we are supposed to hide the fact that we are struggling financially, even though it's the reality for so many of us? The societal pressure to appear financially secure or financially literate can make us feel embarrassed about our lack of money and knowledge.

Yet being broke isn't just about lacking funds in our bank account; it often goes deeper than that, touching on the lack of privilege, missed opportunities, circumstances surrounding your upbringing, and sometimes the absence of money. The way society talks down to people for "being broke" only adds to this burden. It is as if we are expected to pretend to live beyond our means to appease other people and be too ashamed to admit our financial status to seek help or maintain a facade of financial well-being even when we are struggling to make ends meet.

This type of pressure can drive people to overspend while attempting to maintain a lifestyle they can't afford, or exhaust all their resources just to survive. The fear of being seen as financial failures pushes many people to conceal their true financial reality. However, **I do not believe that "being broke" is a result of personal failure.** It's often influenced by larger issues like low wages, discriminatory practices, and inequality (we'll talk more about that later), as well as our personal choices. The stigma surrounding "being broke" blinds us to these issues and prevents broader conversations about them. The idea that everyone can achieve financial success if they "just work hard enough" and "stay disciplined" ignores the reality that many **are** working hard and staying disciplined while navigating the world with far fewer resources.

So where do people who are behind the start line go for financial advice? In 2017, I created an online platform called "The Broke Black Girl," which became a safe space where we could talk about these real money issues without feeling embarrassed. Why was it important for me to create a safe space for personal finance for Black women? Historically, Black women have been underserved in financial education. I wanted to create a space that provided tailored financial guidance, support, and empowerment. I wanted to create a community where Black women could share their experiences, learn from one another, and build confidence in their financial decisions. Financial literacy is nonnegotiable and critical to our survival. I wanted to eliminate the feeling of isolation or inadequacy that comes from being financially uninformed, similar to what I felt around my coworkers many years ago. I wanted to make sure that no Black woman felt excluded or left behind due to a lack of financial knowledge. So what happens when finance is filled with a bunch of confusing terms, phrases, and patriarchal nonsense? It's going to be intimidating, and someone who has never been exposed to that type of terminology is going to want to give up before getting started.

So right there, in a private Facebook group, we tackled real-life financial scenarios like saving with limited income, multigenerational living, generational support versus generational wealth, planning for retirement on a tight budget, navigating public assistance programs, single parenthood finances, five-to-nine gigs after the traditional nine-to-five jobs, rebuilding credit after a setback, and stretching limited resources to make ends meet.

Let's just say the negative perspective surrounding "being broke" found its way into my online community as well, despite how impactful we were. So impactful that in the last few years, through my various platforms, I've reached over forty-two states and ninety-six countries and achieved a membership base of almost half a million women. In addition to my website and social media, I started working with public school systems to offer financial literacy to school-age children and in-person events. I have empowered over three thousand attendees to financially support one hundred–plus Black-woman-owned small businesses, generating more than $100,000 back into my hometown, and an online debt elimination challenge that helped hundreds of women collectively eliminate a debt balance of more than $1,000,000 in forty-five days. Yet still I heard countless voices advising me to drop the word "Broke" from my name. But I refused. "Broke" was my starting point, and I wanted to acknowledge that, and I damn sure wanted people to know that me being Black played a part in that too. I wanted to create a space centered on understanding the reality of your circumstances and creating a personalized plan for growth. This was a space for acknowledgment and acceptance, not defeat. This was me saying, "This is where I am, this is who I am, and that's okay." I was reclaiming my narrative.

In this book, not only will you find practical advice on budgeting, saving, investing, and paying off debt, but I will walk you through my experience with money. From as early as I can remember, every hardship in my life can be traced back to one thing—money. As a Black woman, my financial journey has been uniquely challenging. Together, we're going to go on a journey to dissolve the negative notion of "being broke" and redefine it as a starting point from which we can build and grow.

In *Moving Beyond Broke*, you'll find a mixture of my personal story and practical financial strategies. We'll examine the emotional and psychological aspects of money, the deep-rooted impact societal expectations, cultural backgrounds, and personal beliefs have on our finances, and how our upbringing shapes our financial behaviors and decisions. You'll learn to set realistic financial goals, invest wisely, manage and reduce debt, budget effectively, and save your money. Throughout my story, you'll see how perseverance has been a driving force in overcoming financial barriers and how it can be used to achieve financial stability.

This isn't just a book about numbers; it's about making money less intimidating, redefining what it means to be "broke" and transforming it into a powerful starting point. By leveraging the power of perseverance, you'll discover your inner strength to **move beyond broke** through practical financial advice.

Let's get started.

# CHAPTER 1

# Earning My First Dollar (Budgeting)

**E**xhausted and sweaty from a long day, we gathered around our boss to collect our pay at the end of the night, working a wedding reception for the catering company Lewis Kitchen. I was handed $50 while all the other staff got $75 or $100. I just stood there paralyzed, feeling sick to my stomach. I'd started the day excited about my first real job and thrilled to show off my skills, but I was instantly deflated the moment that crumpled $50 bill hit my palm. Worse still, the boss was my dad.

At the time, I was a twelve-year-old seventh grader who didn't know anything about hourly wages or unfair pay. What I did know was what my dad had always taught me about fairness as a child: treat everyone the same, don't play favorites, and don't take advantage of others. So I couldn't understand why I was paid less than everyone else when I had done the most work.

My dad had always been the cook in our family and used some of his earnings from his restaurant job to launch his own catering company around the time I entered seventh grade. Our family's small apartment filled up with serving utensils and chafing dishes, and I was thrilled when Dad recruited me for the wedding reception, his first gig. I was beyond excited to be working alongside him. I helped him grocery shop, prepare the food, and load the car before we drove to the event together, dressed in my dad's uniform of choice: black pants, a white button-up shirt, and black sneakers.

As the day progressed, Dad moved from giving me important tasks like cooking, displaying the food, and serving guests to assigning me duties like sweeping, washing the dishes, and cleaning up. I didn't know then that I was doing all the chores commonly considered domestic tasks for girls and women. Meanwhile, my male cousins, who made up the rest of the team, spent most of the event carrying boxes, unloading equipment, handling knives, lighting the fire for the chafing dishes, and communicating with the host. I'd practiced all these essential responsibilities with my dad in our own kitchen. For weeks! He knew I could do them well and was more knowledgeable and capable than my cousins, who hadn't received his training. So why did I feel like my dad was trying to keep me out of the way by sticking me with cleaning while my cousins got to do the important work I was much more qualified for?

I couldn't articulate or even identify my emotions back then, but I knew I felt awful. I'd noticed that morning that I was the only girl on staff but had thought nothing of it. I figured my dad built a team based on who would be great for the job. I had no reason to think I'd be treated differently. Until I was.

The time I earned my very first dollar also happened to be the first time I experienced feeling undervalued for my skills and underpaid for my work. The unfair division of labor and unequal pay had me wondering what made us different in my dad's eyes. What was my dad thinking when choosing our tasks and pay? Did he really consider his decisions just, fair, and equal?

I didn't have the courage to ask him.

This wouldn't be the last time I would feel this way, and I know I'm not alone. Women are often afraid to negotiate against unfair pay out of concern that they'll face retaliation or punishment, or the fear that they'll be seen as aggressive or difficult to work with. This fear is often based on societal expectations and stereotypes about how women should act and be treated. There may also be a lack of confidence in their own skills and abilities to negotiate, or a lack of knowledge when it comes to understanding their legal rights in the workplace.

At twelve years old, I wasn't fully aware of practices that impact girls and women simply because of our gender. I worried I would come off ungrateful and disrespectful if I questioned my pay. I felt like I was being punished for something I had no control over. I'd worked harder and longer than anyone that day and believed I deserved more than what I was paid. And because of all this, I couldn't enjoy the money once I received it.

Now that I am much older, a few things cross my mind in an attempt to make sense of why my dad believed $50 was fair. Was it because I was his daughter, so he believed that technically, my financial needs would be met by him anyway? Was it because I was only twelve, and $50 could be considered a lot of money for that age? Was it because my cousins were older than me and more likely to protest unfair pay? Or was it because my work was considered less important and expected of me because I was a girl, and $50 was my father being generous? **I believed it to be the latter, which sat with me for years.**

I was triggered to later learn that girls start experiencing pay discrepancies early in childhood, with boys being paid twice as much weekly allowance as girls.[1] As an adult today, I can honestly say I do not believe my dad underpaid me with malicious intent or even

---

1    https://www.chicagotribune.com/lifestyles/ct-life-kids-allowance-gender-gap20180803-story.html.

thought about it as deeply as I did, but that's the thing with patriarchal beliefs: they are so deeply ingrained in society's everyday practices that even something as innocent as earning my first dollar while working for my father's business could not escape their influence. But here's the thing: we are not bound by these ingrained practices and the limitations imposed on us, but by our relentless pursuit of equity, equality, and empowerment. Every setback, every challenge, and every inequity faced is a testament to our strength and perseverance. The history we are up against is intimidating, I know, but it is also the very force that fuels our determination to knock down every barrier (person, place, or practice) that gets in the way of our financial stability. Every step we take toward financial empowerment is a victory won against systemic structures that have tried to hold us back.

## We're Up Against History

Unfortunately, my experience with my dad was not unique. Women have been subjected to wage and workplace discrimination for generations, and we still are today. In the nineteenth and twentieth centuries, women were restricted to low-paying jobs and earned less than men while doing the same work. Our entry into paid employment has played a major role in the growth of our economy. But even still, the wage gap continues. Currently, white women earn eighty-three cents for every dollar a white man earns,[2] and Black women earn sixty-three cents for every dollar a white man earns.[3]

Black women have historically faced economic challenges, including wage inequities, limited access to credit, and disproportionate burdens of unpaid work and labor. Despite these challenges, Black women have demonstrated financial resilience and resourcefulness, but that rarely comes easy.

---

2   https://www.payscale.com/research-and-insights/gender-pay-gap/#module-15.

3   https://hbr.org/2021/08/black-women-arent-paid-fairly-and-it-starts-as-early-as-age-16.

Although I would like to believe that times have changed since my experience with my dad twenty years ago, society has not made much progress when it comes to women and money. It's been only fifty years since the Equal Credit Opportunity Act was established in 1974, making it unlawful for lenders to discriminate against women.[4] The Women's Business Ownership Act wasn't signed into law until thirty-five short years ago in 1988, the same year I was born, eliminating laws that required women to have their husband or a male family member sign their business loans.[5]

It may sound like a bunch of legal jargon when we talk about laws and acts being established and passed, but when we attach real people and real scenarios to them, we get a better understanding of how detrimental some of those patriarchal laws have been to women well after they were terminated. Sixty years ago, if my grandmother wanted to purchase a home or take out any line of credit, she would have needed her husband, father, brother, or even her son to cosign for her, even if her own financial statements proved that she indeed could have covered the line of credit on her own.

This means women have had only less than one generation to take advantage of most opportunities to earn an income and build wealth for ourselves and our families. Even still, we are met with many other adversities, in and out of the workforce. Meanwhile, men have had centuries to build wealth and pass it down, further widening the income and wealth gap between the sexes. The obstacles to earning a sufficient income only increase for Black women. Black women lose close to a million dollars over the course of a forty-year career because of unfair pay practices.[6] That's an additional $25,000 per year that could have gone to saving, investing,

---

4   https://www.ecfr.gov/current/title-12/chapter-X/part-1002#1002.2.

5   https://www.congress.gov/bill/100th-congress/house-bill/5050.

6   https://leanin.org/data-about-the-gender-pay-gap-for-black-women.

increasing our quality of life, reliable transportation, healthier food choices, better childcare and education for our kids, and being able to take on the jobs we want instead of the jobs we need. While being paid unfairly, Black women are still expected to financially cover the same expenses as our non-Black counterparts, but from much smaller paychecks.

Discussions about the gender wage gap are important, but they're not enough. I'm talking about the systematic, financial oppression of women of color throughout history. Black women have borne the brunt of generations of gender and race discrimination in every aspect of wealth building and financial freedom—from being considered property to being blocked from owning property, redlined in the housing market and sidelined in the workplace, constantly overworked and underpaid while being told to be grateful for crumbs falling off the table while being denied a seat.

## Reclaiming Our Right to Be Financially Free

I know these harsh statistics can make an already difficult situation feel worse. But stay with me. I wrote this book to help Black women thrive despite the financial limitations we face, and to do that, it helps to know the facts so we can rise above them. The truth is that women are most likely to experience pay inequality in the workplace, in every country, and in every industry. The median income for young Black women between twenty and twenty-nine years old in America is only $21,400 per year.[7] Now, I'm referring to earned income here, which is the money that you get from any work that you perform, whether that's from your employer or self-employment as a business owner. This looks like hourly wages, salaries, bonuses, commission pay, tips, or any net earning from gig work.

---

7    https://www.ssa.gov/policy/docs/factsheets/at-a-glance/earnings-women-age-race-ethnicity.html.

The key word to focus on here is "earned." The definition of "earned" here is to obtain money in exchange for labor or services. In other words, you get money for the work that you put in. Everyone has the right to be paid fairly for the work they do. I first felt the sting of pay inequality when working for my dad. At the time that injustice hurt emotionally, although aside from having less spending money in my pocket, it didn't harm me logistically. My parents covered my basic needs. But raising girls in a world where pay inequality is the status quo sets us up for a lifetime of undue struggle.

Earned income determines most people's ability to meet their basic needs. This poses a big challenge for so many Black women, who face a wider pay gap despite participating in the workforce at a much higher rate than any other women.[8] Most of our experience with money exists at the intersectionality of sexism and racism, and this upholds harmful practices that work directly against our ability to earn a sufficient wage. We are often left working twice as hard for half the pay while still trying to maintain a household and manage our finances with much smaller opportunities. Pay inequality leads to women having fewer financial resources to support themselves and their families. It also makes it extremely difficult for them to achieve financial independence. Add to all this that, statistically, women are expected to live longer than men. Longevity paired with low income means women must continuously find strategic and relevant methods to do more with less.

When you are paid less than you are worth, trying to thrive financially is like running up a down escalator. It doesn't mean anyone in this situation is stuck forever, but we need to take action to break out of this cycle.

Looking at the big picture, **we need to teach our young girls the power of negotiating as early as possible.** When I got my first taste of

---

8    https://blog.dol.gov/2021/08/03/5-facts-about-black-women-in-the-labor-force.

unfair pay at twelve years old, I didn't have the words to describe what I was feeling. But now as an adult, I truly believe that had I had more encouragement to be confident and assertive, it would have empowered me to speak up for myself or at least ask why and put the responsibility of making sense of this back on my father instead of myself. When girls and women learn to negotiate, they become changemakers, actively shaping their own financial futures.

That said, it's important to note that while teaching young girls to negotiate is essential, it should not be their sole responsibility to ensure they receive fair treatment. Systems and policies should be in place to ensure that girls and women are not discriminated against and are given equal opportunities. Negotiation skills are just one tool that girls and women can use to help level the playing field, but it's also critical that we work toward systemic change.

But systemic changes take a long time. As we teach our girls to stand up for their financial rights, and we push for a world wherein they won't have to fight for those rights, we need to take control of our financial futures now. We can do this despite the history we were raised in or the forces working against us today. This entire book is designed to help you do exactly that. We do not have to be bound by the constraints of our circumstances.

I've started this book with a spotlight on income because the first step to reclaiming your financial future is to pay close attention to your income and spending. Yes, everything is harder when income is limited. But it's still essential to have a spending strategy while you work on growing your income. Looking back at my family's money situation, it's clear to me that this was missing from my parents' financial picture.

When I was growing up, my parents did not discuss finances with my siblings and me. Still, in a small two-bedroom apartment, you are bound to see and overhear things, and those things made me curious about our financial situation. I would overhear my dad complain about the cost of certain things, and this made me believe we didn't have a lot of money. There would be times when we would have to shop at the discount store for groceries, and even then, Dad would complain about the prices. Other times, my parents would be so low on funds that they'd have to get household items like toilet tissue or light bulbs from the corner store, where they were often three times the price, with a promise to pay later. Yet in the same week, Dad would buy every kid in our neighborhood, including all four of his children, popsicles when the ice cream truck drove down our street. Don't get me wrong—I love this memory of him. It reminds me of what a big heart he had even through tough times. But his contradictory financial behaviors confused me. They made me question the seriousness of his financial complaints or whether money really was an issue like he made it seem.

Looking back now, it's clear to me that my parents were struggling with two very real financial limitations:

1. **They were trying to support four kids on a very low income.**
   Growing up, every adult I knew worked a service-based job that did not pay well. I remember waking up as my dad left the house before dawn to make it to the barbeque restaurant he worked for, or begging my mom to let me stay up late to wait for my grandma to come home from her job at the local nursing home. I didn't fully understand it as a kid, but it was very difficult for my parents to make ends meet as a family of six with jobs like these. They were stuck in a cycle of waiting for payday and, even then, not having enough to cover the basic necessities.

2. **They did not have the financial tools to change their situation.**
   Nor did they have the educational resources to learn more. Despite those barriers, they tried. My dad's attempt to launch Lewis Kitchen was full of optimism, but he never managed to grow it

into a profitable business. I believe things could have turned out differently for our whole family if my parents had had a better understanding of how to manage and grow their money, both personally and professionally.

It's hard to break out of a challenging money situation without tools to help you rise above whatever limitations you're facing. And the first one you need is one of the most powerful ways to take action—and the most basic: a budget to track your income and spending.

## Your First Financial Tool: A Budget

It's possible my dad had budgeted some cash to treat us kids to the ice cream truck whenever he pleased, but knowing what I do now about my parents' financial situation back then, it's unlikely. The more probable truth is that he was spending from the heart because he wanted to give his kids joy on a summer afternoon. That was my dad—spend it today and figure the rest out tomorrow. As a parent myself, I get it. There's so much beauty in wanting to make your children happy during tough times. But it's also confusing for a child to witness, especially a child who is curious about money, when spending that $8 on ice cream meant he might have to cut corners on something else later.

I'm not judging my dad for buying us ice cream when times were tough. Actually, that gesture captures one of the most important parts of budgeting that I encourage everyone to do: make room in your budget to spend on things that make you feel good—whether it's ice cream for your kids, monthly salon visits, or dinner with friends. Even when money is tight. *Especially* when money is tight. Doing this will keep you motivated to stick to budgeting and let you spend in a way that won't harm your larger financial goals. It also debunks one of the biggest myths about budgeting that stops most people from ever getting started: that budgeting is restrictive.

The first time I heard the word "budget," it felt like a punishment because it seemed so limiting. Yet the more I learned about budgeting, I understood that it is one of the most liberating financial tools you can use. Let me say it again: your budget is not a punishment for overspending—it's the foundation for creating the life you want by spending money intentionally in service of your goals and aligned with your values. Creating a budget puts you in full control, which is especially important when your income is limited. We don't always have control over how much money we make, but we do have control over how we spend the money we earn. Even on a very limited income, a budget allows you to set aside at least some money for small luxuries (yes, you *can* have your double latte with extra whip), save for bigger splurges over time (holidays and trips), and eventually reach your most audacious financial goals (buying your first home or traveling the world for a year).

If my parents had budgeted, my dad would have known that on some weeks, his dollars would have served him better if he'd put them toward saving for a rainy day; other weeks, there was enough cash to put toward treats for the kids. And once they'd budgeted long enough, they probably would have had enough control over their finances to have a regular flow of cash for spontaneous spending or possibly a better understanding of exactly where they stood financially. They wouldn't have had to lose as many precious dollars to high interest payments. Maybe they could have even saved and invested some. But they did their best with what they had and what they knew; in their own way, they did teach me how powerful intentional spending can be.

My mom has always said you have to work with what you've got. That's exactly what we're doing when we budget. We're making the money we have work for us in a way that moves us toward our financial goals. I know it can seem ridiculous to even think about budgeting when your income is low, but one thing you'll quickly realize about money management is that the habits we create around the earned income we have access to, both now and in the future, are the biggest contributor to our success. Our mindset matters much more than how much we have in the bank at any given time.

So let's wrap our minds around budgeting. I like to think of finances as laying the foundation of a house. Before you can build your dream house, you first have to make sure the foundation you build your house on is solid. The key to having a sufficient foundation is not to allow your total monthly expenses to exceed your monthly income. And I get it; that's easier said than done, and we'll talk more about that throughout this book. For now, it helps to know that your budget is the support system for every other floor or room you want to add to your financial house. Before you can decide if you want to save, invest, take a vacation, or buy a new outfit, your budget must be strong enough to carry the weight of those new expenses. If your expenses start to exceed your income, the foundation—your budget—becomes weak and can put the entire house at risk of crumbling.

## Let's Build Your Budget Blueprint

So how do you make sure that your budget is balanced and the foundation is solid? Before you start laying the foundation, you have to create the blueprint. The blueprint is the plan you'll create after getting clear on your income, expenses, financial goals, and habits. This plan will outline how you will manage your finances and serve as a guide to achieve your financial goals.

Start by taking an honest look at your income and expenses. The key here is to take an *honest* look. Many budgets are unrealistic because they're built on assumptions and goals that are overly optimistic. It's too easy to hope that our bills will be the same each month or that our income will be more than it is. Many people also create budgets based on estimations of how much money they will save, which in many cases turns out to be less than what they'd anticipated. All those factors play into creating an unrealistic budget.

So let's put aside any assumptions and estimates and look at real dollars to create your budget blueprint. We'll start with your income. Gather all your **reliable income sources** (that is, income that you will receive 100 percent for sure), such as your salary, side hustles, child support, alimony, etc. Statistically, more than 72 percent of parents raising kids with nonresidential parents do not receive child support at all.[9] Of the 28 percent of parents who do receive child support, a third only get sporadic or irregular payments, so if child support is not money you can absolutely count on, don't factor it into your monthly budget. Factoring in irregular income can make your budget unpredictable. Instead focus on calculating your baseline income. Determine the minimum amount you can depend on each month. This baseline should be used to cover your essential expenses, helping keep your budget intact despite any fluctuations in your income.

Open a spreadsheet and create a line item for each monthly income source and the amount. If any of them fluctuates, like income based on an hourly schedule that changes each week or flexible gig work, look at that income source's trend over the course of several months (or however much data you have) and put a number that represents its average. For example, if a side hustle earned you $600 in January, $200 in February, $300 in March, and $500 in April, put $400 in that income source's line—at least for your blueprint. Remember, we're starting out by creating a plan for your budget so you have a sense of what you can afford. The budget you use to track day-to-day spending will be based on the real dollars that go in and out of your bank account each week. We'll get to that in a minute. For now, write down all your reliable income sources and the monthly amount for each.

Next, calculate your **monthly expenses**. This is often a rude awakening for many people. Start by making a list of your **fixed monthly**

9   https://www.census.gov/library/publications/2022/demo/p70-176.html.
    https://www.census.gov/content/dam/Census/library/publications/2022/demo/p70-176.pdf.

**expenses.** These are bills that usually stay the same each month, like rent, mortgage, and loan payments. Next, make a list of your **variable monthly expenses.** These are expenses that you still pay monthly but that fluctuate from month to month. Variable expenses include groceries, personal care, utilities, home or car repairs, and entertainment.

We would like to believe we don't spend as much money as we actually do, and it can be shocking to realize how much small purchases add up. No—I'm not about to lecture you to cut out your daily coffee if that's your thing. Keep small joys if you can factor them into your budget. I'm talking about the purchases we need just to get by. They add up fast, whether they're routine items or unexpected. In my household of three, we easily spend $100 a week on our big grocery run, and then another $50 to $75 on quick trips to the store to replenish essentials like bread for school lunches, peanut butter, batteries for my son's dead Xbox game controller, or ginger ale for the stomach bug my twelve-year-old brought home from school for the fifth time. There is always something we didn't expect we'd be buying in a given week. More often than not, if you are not tracking your expenses regularly, these expenses can add up over time and push you over your budget. We need to expect the unexpected if we want a real, honest budget. Sometimes what we consider unexpected expenses are things we can anticipate if we take a closer look at our patterns and circumstances. Car repairs, medical bills, and home maintenance are not entirely unforeseeable—they are a part of life. By acknowledging that these things are likely to happen and planning for them, we shift our mindset and habits from being reactive to proactive.

## Don't Forget to Factor in Annual Expenses

Maybe this has happened to you: It's the middle of the month and you're feeling pretty good about your finances. Your rent and utilities are paid; you sent in your credit card payment; your fridge is full; you even have enough cash on hand for takeout on Friday night. Then, *boom!* You get an email that your annual car insurance bill is due in two weeks. That's $600 you need to pay out of thin air. Suddenly, you're not feeling so good about your finances anymore. We've all been there. But the thing about these surprise bills is that they're not really surprises. They're often just not on our radar until they're due.

Factoring in annual expenses is an important piece to creating a budget that accurately reflects your financial situation. These are expenses that accrue once a year, such as property taxes, vehicle registrations, insurance premiums, summer programs for your children, subscription fees, and holiday expenses. They can be easily overlooked, and failing to account for them in your budget can lead to financial stress and feeling overwhelmed when those bills are due. Annual expenses are usually much more expensive and harder to cover out of pocket within the same month that they are due.

To factor annual expenses into your monthly budget, divide each expense by twelve to decide how much money you should put to the side each month in your budget. That $600 car insurance bill breaks down to $50 a month. If you'd like, you can create a separate savings account for annual expenses and put money into that account each month, to be used only when it's time to pay those bills. By taking the time to plan for these expenses, you can avoid feeling overwhelmed when they land and have peace of mind knowing that you've prepared in advance.

## Fact-Check Your Blueprint

Before you do any other number crunching, you have to fact-check your income and expenses. Compare the income sources and monthly expenses against your actual spending, which can be found in your financial documents like bank and credit card statements. This is a sure way to get a better understanding of exactly where your money is going. Review your financial statements line by line for the last three to six months. That is a good enough time frame to determine your true spending habits and expenses. Organize each transaction into different categories like housing, food, transportation, personal care, entertainment, etc. Some banks have free online tools that analyze your spending for you and even show you a pie chart that breaks down your spending categories (more on banking tools in chapter 3). Once you have a clear sense of your spending, adjust your blueprint as necessary. Then subtract your expenses from your income to determine how they work together and where you might need to change.

## Time to Get Real: Working with Your Real-Time Budget

Your blueprint is a starting point to help you figure out where you stand financially so you can create a realistic budget. If you find that your reliable income is, say, $3,000 a month, but in fact-checking you find you spend more like $4,000 a month, your real-time budget needs an adjustment. In other words, you either need to find a way to get your monthly income up to $4,000 to cover your expenses or find a way to get your monthly expenses down to $3,000 so you're not spending more than you have. This is essential to financial security. You may be able to live beyond your means for a short time by dipping into savings to cover expenses, or by racking up credit card debt, but this is not sustainable, and it's the opposite of wealth building.

Having a budget is usually the first financial tool I recommend, since it's what will help you keep your income and expenses synced. Creating a budget may seem overwhelming, but once you get started, I promise it will be empowering to see where your money goes as you gain control over your income and expenses. And while a lot of people find it challenging to create and follow one, I'm going to ask you to create four, a budget for different phases. Yep—don't worry, this is worth it. If I'm going to teach you how to budget, I'll teach you the way that has worked best for me. I swear it's a lot less painful than it sounds, and it will give you peace of mind in the future. I'll walk you through the steps for creating your budget in the worksheet at the end of this chapter. For now, let's look at each type of budget I recommend.

## Four Types of Budgets

Being a single mom comes with financial challenges, but I've found a way to navigate them by creating four different budgets to alternate between depending on my household's needs. Besides different life phases and situations requiring budget adjustments, this practice of custom-creating different budgets ahead of time gives me incredible peace of mind when shit hits the fan. Why? Because one of the hardest things to do when you're in the middle of a crisis is having to figure out your finances while trying to survive.

These are the four budgets I rotate between, but you can create fewer or more based on your specific circumstances and lifestyle:

### 1. REGULAR BUDGET—YOUR FINANCIAL BACKBONE

This comprehensive budget includes all essential and nonessential expenses like rent, groceries, and utility bills. This budget helps me keep track of our daily spending and ensures a balanced financial lifestyle.

### 2. SEASONAL BUDGET

Both of my boys are student athletes, so expenses can add up quickly. This dedicated budget allows me to allocate funds specifically for my boys' academic and athletic needs, like equipment, camp fees, and tutoring. The reason for this separate budget is that these expenses fluctuate throughout the year, with the athletic seasons and academic sessions taking a toll on my finances. For you, this dedicated budget may be something different—perhaps holiday spending, travel, a specific hobby or event that tends to take over your budget at certain times of the year.

### 3. IF EVERYTHING GOES TO SHIT BUDGET

Life can throw unexpected curveballs, whether you lose your job, get divorced, or have a car accident, so having a contingency plan is important. This emergency budget drastically reduces our living expenses to the bare minimum, allowing us to weather tough times without compromising our basic needs. This essentials-only budget gives me peace of mind, knowing I have a plan for financial resilience during rough patches that allows us to navigate emergencies while covering food, housing, utilities, medication, transportation, basic clothing and hygiene items, childcare, and insurance. Your essentials will be slightly different, but make sure you include only your absolute bare necessities.

### 4. DEBT AND SAVINGS BUDGET

When I need to prioritize paying off debt and saving for a major expense, I switch to this budget that helps me temporarily focus on these narrow goals to allocate more resources and accelerate my progress. This budget goes beyond the monthly savings, investing, and debt payments in my regular budget by gaining momentum on targeted goals like paying off a car loan, credit card debt, saving for a vacation, or making a down payment.

Do four budgets still sound like overkill to you? You may not need them all, but I've found it works extremely well for me to be proactive and have room to be financially flexible in different stages of life and emergency situations without jeopardizing our quality of life. The beauty of customized budgets allows me to adapt to changing circumstances as soon as they happen, because I have these budgets ready and waiting to go, instead of scrambling to meet changing needs efficiently.

Do you need a fancy, complicated budgeting app for this? Absolutely not. I recommend creating a simple spreadsheet, or if Excel makes you want to pound your head against the wall, use paper and pen. I don't suggest apps, because they eliminate the hands-on act of learning how to manage your finances versus relying on someone or something else to gather your information, categorize it, interpret it, and tell you what to do with it. If you do the initial heavy lifting of digging into your financial data, you're already ahead of most app users.

## Identifying Room for Change

Many factors can impact your budget, including your income, spending and lifestyle habits, your employer, and outside factors such as inflation, the job market, and policies that affect housing and childcare costs. There is power in knowing where your money is going. By taking a proactive approach to your budget and identifying areas of improvement where you can make change, you are putting yourself in a better position to improve your situation and have more control over your money.

One way to identify changes in your budget is to look for ways to increase your income or decrease your spending. Decreasing your spending looks like reviewing your spending habits and finding ways to cut back on your expenses or saving money in other areas by opting for cheaper alternatives. Increasing your income can involve negotiating for a raise at work or doing side gigs to bring in extra income.

## Maximizing Your Income

Maximizing your income is important to establishing financial stability. Yet with a limited amount of money, time, and resources, it can be difficult to know where to start.

Setting a budget gives you a clear idea of your financial situation so you can set realistic goals to get you where you want to be. You can consider further training in your field through certifications or a career change or start smaller. Look for ways to maximize your income by advocating for your financial interests, such as negotiating a lower interest rate with your credit card company or applying for financial assistance programs that your service providers may offer.

You can also maximize earnings through your employer. Going back to my first corporate job at nineteen, I had no clue how to go about negotiating a better salary and taking advantage of my company's retirement options, including matching my 401(k) contributions (more on all this in later chapters). Your job may also offer perks such as career advancement or continuing education, childcare, gym memberships, or benefits through partner organizations.

Now that we've discussed the theory of how to negotiate, calculate, track, and maximize your income, it's time to build your first budget to look at your expenses and spending habits. Aside from, well, having an income in the first place, this is the foundation of money management and wealth building, because it teaches you how to make every dollar work toward your financial goals.

## Zero-Based Budgeting for the Win

I recommend what's commonly known as "zero-based budgeting." With this approach, you assign a job to every dollar in your bank account so that your income equals your "expenses." Now, I put "expenses" in quotation marks because with zero-based budgeting, investments, savings, and debt payments are treated like monthly expenses. They'll have a line item in your budget just like your vehicle payment or electric bill, and you'll assign money to them just like you would any other expense. Only *after* you've assigned money to meet your savings, investing, and/ or debt-payoff goals will you assign money to less essential expenses. Always pay yourself first. If you don't do this, your money will run away before you ever know what happened to it, and you'll constantly wonder why you can't seem to get ahead financially.

Here's how it works:

1. **Align Your Budget with Big-Picture Goals:** Your foundation must always be ensuring that your budget reflects your personal values and financial goals, which will shift seasonally throughout the

year and depend on your specific phase of life. Your budget is not a punishment for overspending but a way to create the life you want. For example, if you aim to save for a down payment on a house, you might prioritize savings over less essential spending. This is where you could use your custom Debt and Savings Budget rather than your regular one.

2. **Start Each Month at Zero:** Begin each month with a budget where your income minus your expenses equals zero. Every dollar you earn that month must be assigned a specific purpose, whether it's for expenses, savings, investments, or debt repayment. Your budget should equal zero after subtracting your expenses from your income.

3. **Justify Every Expense:** For each new budget period (usually a month), evaluate each expense category. Just because you spent money on something last month doesn't mean you should include it in the next month's budget. Ask yourself if each expense is necessary and contributes to your financial goals.

4. **Prioritize Your Spending:** Rank your expenses in order of importance. Essentials like your rent, mortgage, utilities, groceries, transportation, and debt payments will top the list, while discretionary expenses like dining out, entertainment, and luxury items will be lower on the list. This part is where your four different types of budgets come into play. If cash is low in a particular month, your discretionary expenses need to be minimal so that you can cover your essential expenses.

5. **Adapt to Changes:** Zero-based budgeting provides flexibility to adjust your budget as your financial situation changes. Sometimes, you won't need to alternate between your four different

budgets but could make a smaller calibration. For example, if you get a raise, decide how to allocate the extra income. If expenses rise, determine where to cut back.

6. **Detailed Tracking:** Keep a detailed record of your expenses on paper, in your spreadsheet, or using your bank's online categories. This will help you identify areas where you might be overspending and need to cut back.

7. **Regular Reviews:** At the end of each month, review your budget. Did you stick to it? If not, understand why and adjust the next month's budget accordingly. Do this for three to six months to gain a deeper understanding of where each dollar goes.

Zero-based budgeting requires discipline and ongoing attention, but it also encourages a proactive approach to managing money, ensuring that your financial resources are used efficiently and in alignment with your personal goals and priorities. Zero-based budgeting has transformed my finances because I learned it's about much more than cutting expenses. I love the idea of assigning every dollar a job, making it work toward something that truly matters to *me*, rather than wondering where all my money went at the end of each month. I now make my money work as hard as I do.

## How to Create Your First Budget—Worksheet

Before diving into building your first budget, make sure you've gone through the three main steps of creating your budget blueprint:

1. **Open a spreadsheet and create a line item for each monthly income source (alternatively use paper and pen).**
   To do this, take an honest look at your income. Many budgets are unrealistic, too optimistic, and therefore pointless. Like

you, your budget must live and work in reality. Gather all your information about reliable income sources you'll receive for sure (salaries, wages, regular side gigs, self-employment income based on your tax returns, not wishful thinking). Be careful about including income sources that are often irregular or sporadic, such as child support, royalties, commissions, tips, etc. If any of them fluctuates based on your hourly schedule, for example, take the average you've received over six months (or however much data you have).

2. **Now calculate your monthly expenses and create a line item for each.**
   Start with your fixed expenses, such as rent, mortgage, or car loans. Then add your variable monthly expenses, such as groceries, personal care items, home maintenance, or gas and car repairs. Remember your annual expenses, too, like your annual car registration, property taxes, subscription fees, or holiday gifts. Divide all these annual fees by twelve and add the partial expense to your monthly budget.

3. **Fact-check your blueprint.**
   Compare your income sources and monthly spending line items against your actual spending by reviewing your bank and credit card statements, and categorize each transaction into housing, food, entertainment, etc. Most online banking services offer this function.

Budgeting is not a punishment for overspending. It's a gift you give yourself to ensure your money works as hard as you do.

# CHAPTER 2

# Money Looks Better in the Bank (Saving)

had a lot going on when I was sixteen years old. I was a typical teen in most ways: I loved spending time with my close group of friends. We spent a lot of our free time hanging out at the mall, going from store to store without a particular goal in mind. It was less about shopping and more about being together. It was our go-to spot and a place where we could see and be seen and occasionally buy something with the little money we had. Our neighborhoods and each of our houses were also regular and **free** hangout spots. We would get together to just chill and gossip about our day. These get-togethers were simple and didn't require much money. On the weekends, we would usually go to a teen club or to the movies. We would pool our money together for food and entry fees just to make sure our whole group got in on the fun regardless of who had money. This period of my life was marked by simplicity in how we chose to spend our time and money. Schoolwork also kept me busy. After spending eight to ten hours at school (factoring in traveling to and from), I often had a few hours' worth of homework in the evenings. I also decided to take night classes for extra help after realizing that math was not my strong suit (ironic, I know). I took my academics seriously and was always striving to improve my grades.

But there was more to my life than school and friends. My family was going through a transitional period at that time. We went from a two-parent household to a one-parent household, and my mom worked long hours to make ends meet. I was the oldest of six siblings (four of us lived in the same home), and after school, I had to pick up my younger siblings from school, get them home, and make sure they did their homework. By sixteen, I knew how to grocery shop, use public transportation to get just about anywhere within St. Louis, write a check to pay bills, and get dinner started before my mom came home from work. At times this meant missing out on my after-school programs, doubling up on homework assignments, or canceling on my friends. It was a lot of work, but I loved my siblings and wanted to do everything possible to help.

With all this going on, I was shocked when, a few months after my sixteenth birthday, my mom suggested I look for a job. Getting a job during high school had never been on my agenda, and quite frankly, I was offended that she even suggested it. But her awful advice (to my teenage mind) went beyond the job. She also encouraged me to save $20 a week out of every paycheck for a "rainy day." I hated this idea.

I did get a part-time cashier job at Burlington Coat Factory because it felt like the coming-of-age thing to do, and I was excited to finally have money that I could spend on whatever I wanted. Back then, my priorities were expenses like movie tickets, shopping at Forever 21 or American Eagle, and buying every pair of Jordans that came out. But I still resisted the idea of saving $20 from each paycheck. Not only did it seem like an insignificant amount to save in the grand scheme of things, but it felt like a lot to cut out of each paycheck when I was working so hard physically and mentally to earn $6.50 an hour. I barely brought home $100 a week after taxes. I had never realized how tiring working in retail could be. I had been to this store hundreds of times with my mother before working there, and it never occurred to me how hard the employees worked. The constant moving, noise, and taking orders from my boss and coworkers left me feeling exhausted at the end of each shift. This seemed counterintuitive to me, even as a sixteen-year-old, but I found most things at that job to be new and shocking. I remember crying in the bathroom on my first day because I had no idea what any of the onboarding paperwork meant that my supervisor required me to sign. How is a sixteen-year-old supposed to know what a W-4 form is? Was I signing my life away? I got through it, but it was an overwhelming experience.

After all that stress, I felt entitled to the freedom to spend the little money I earned however I pleased. Saving it for something that might never happen just didn't make sense to me. So I didn't do it.

## Dream Big, Think Small

It turns out that ignoring my mom's advice cost me $49,112.73. That's the amount I would have accumulated by age thirty-five, if I'd listened to her at sixteen and saved $20 a week (or $80 a month), because of a magical phenomenon known as *compound interest*, which is basically the "eighth wonder of the world," according to none other than infamous physicist Albert Einstein. Compound interest means that you're earning interest not only on the money you've invested (*principal*) but also on the interest that your investment earns over time. By comparison, only saving that money without investing it and earning compound interest at an average annual rate of 10 percent would amount to $18,240. Still a nice chunk of change, but nothing like $49,112.73.

Unfortunately, my mindset didn't just stop me from saving those $20. I carried it into adulthood and skipped numerous opportunities to save and secure my financial future. I believed that I needed to have large sums of money to make saving worthwhile. Whether it was passing up on employer-matched retirement contributions, saving my spare change, failing to establish an emergency fund, or overlooking opportunities to invest in my future, my beliefs about saving caused me to miss out on the potential growth and security that could have been achieved through disciplined saving.

My big oversight was that I didn't realize my mom was **dreaming big and thinking small**. Dreaming big meant envisioning a future when I would have a strong foundation of financial stability and responsibility. Thinking small involved breaking down that vision into small, actionable steps. By encouraging me to start working at sixteen and save even a small amount from each paycheck, my mom was teaching me the importance of building strong financial habits early on and the power that consistent, small efforts can have over time. Dream big, think small is the ultimate example of perseverance in personal finance, and it's so powerful.

I eventually realized that my mom was right all along. The realization hit even harder when I considered the additional challenges my mom knew I was likely to face as a woman navigating the workforce. She understood from her own experience the importance of leveraging time as a driving factor, especially when income is limited. My mother recognized that financial security wasn't a guarantee for everyone in a society plagued by income inequality, and rather than ignore this, she was trying to teach me a valuable lesson: be proactive. She knew that the deck was often going to be stacked against individuals like me, and that incremental savings is an essential tool for overcoming those barriers. By leveraging time as a driving factor, she knew that even limited income could be transformed into a powerful force for change.

## To Be Fair, We Were Both Right

I didn't understand the significance of my mom's wisdom about saving money until I was in my thirties. But I have to be fair to sixteen-year-old Dasha. She wasn't entirely wrong. Part of my struggle to connect with my mom's advice was that the reason she'd suggested I save didn't mean anything to me. It wasn't *my big* dream, because I had no clue what a "rainy day" could be. I really didn't understand the concept, because financial challenges were normal for me, and if I happened to have a rainy day in the future, I believed my parents would be my umbrella.

And since the big dream wasn't personally motivating to me, the small act didn't seem worth it. It felt like too much to give up $20 of the tiny paycheck I'd busted my butt to earn when my teenage lifestyle had so many important expenses.

I'm not blaming my mom for suggesting I save for a rainy day. She was right. I just wish I'd seen the bigger picture behind her advice: incremental saving is the secret to achieving money goals. I just needed to see how it could help *me* achieve *my goals.* Twenty dollars a week, for five years, would have been $5,200 in the bank when I turned twenty-one. That could have given me the financial stability to put a down payment on a vehicle. Even $20 a week after one year would have been $1,040. That's a huge sum of money for a seventeen-year-old. I could have taken a nice vacation with my friends to celebrate graduating high school or used it to put down a security deposit on my first apartment. Saving $20 per week wouldn't have felt so painful or insignificant if I'd taken the time to do the math and then attach the numbers to my own big dream.

It's easy to dismiss a teen whose main concern is having enough cash for movie popcorn and sneakers. But the truth is, my childhood resistance to saving captured something people can struggle with at any age: **When income is limited and expenses are overwhelming, saving can seem impossible.** This is especially true when you're already working hard to stretch every dollar. Tucking away $20 for a potential future problem doesn't make sense when you need that money for something very real right now. As a teen with adult-level responsibilities, I was fiercely protective of those few extra dollars that helped me enjoy some carefree time with my friends. My paycheck was so small, and there was so much I wanted to do in the present, that it felt there wasn't anything left to dream big with. That kind of planning just wasn't for me; not when I had so little money to work with.

In retrospect, I'm glad I was wrong. Dreaming big *is* for everyone, and thinking small is one of the most powerful and underrated ways to get there. Now, more than a decade later, I leverage dreaming big and acting small all the time. I recently set up a joint high-yield savings account with my sister with automatic weekly payments from both of us. These small payments don't take away from our regular financial responsibilities, but we'll still save enough to cover the expenses for one trip together every year. We've been joking about wishing we could be roommates again, but this will do! It's our little rebellion against the regular routine of our lives and a fun sisterly pact that makes us both excited about saving small amounts over the entire year. Talking about savings usually sounds so serious, but it can also be about building up a fund for something that'll give you a little piece of happiness, a break from your regular routine, and beautiful memories—especially if you're sharing the dream with someone you adore.

## Dreaming Big Is for Everyone

Everyone deserves to dream big. I'll say that again, and a little louder, in case you thought I wasn't talking to you: **everyone deserves to dream big**. If you're reading this at a time in your life when money is tight and saving feels impossible, this message is especially for you. And let me be clear: dreaming big doesn't have to look like a Range Rover in your driveway and a Birkin bag on your arm. Actually, it rarely looks like that. Dreaming big is as simple as having the financial security of knowing you can afford something that's important to you.

Don't let the size of your goal intimidate you into inaction. Incremental saving will eventually get you to achieve that big financial goal. It doesn't look like it at first, but I promise this approach works. Sometimes, people get so focused on the idea they're not doing enough that they end up doing nothing at all. If you're discouraged because you can't save $1,000 right away, remember to break it down into saving $20 fifty times. Taking small steps over time can lead to big achievements. This approach doesn't just make the end goal seem more attainable, it can also work wonders for your stress levels. I'm less likely to feel overwhelmed and able to celebrate small savings victories along the way, which keeps me motivated. I've been guiding myself through this journey with manageable steps, rather than a single intimidating leap, and I haven't missed with this method yet.

### Low-Effort Ways to Save Up to $1,000

Incremental savings, or "working with what you've got," as my mom put it, involves consistently setting aside small amounts of money over an extended period of time and allowing it to accumulate gradually. It's not about saving huge amounts of money at once but making regular contributions, no matter how small they may seem. Consider it as building a financial safety net. A safety net is made up of numerous individual threads woven together, each thread representing a small contribution. Even the tiniest amounts can gradually build up a strong safety net over time. By consistently setting aside small sums of money, you are reinforcing and strengthening your financial safety net. And you can rely on that safety net to fund whatever is important to you.

If you're not sure how to start with incremental saving, or how to fit it into your life, here are some simple strategies to try.

1. **Automated Weekly Transfers:** This is how I'm saving for the annual vacation with my sister. Save $20 per week in a high-yield savings account. Annual Savings: $1,040.

2. **Gradual Savings Plan:** Start with $1 and increase the amount weekly. I'll get into the details of these plans and savings chal-

lenges I've run with my social media followers later in this chapter. Annual Savings: $1,378.

3. **Round-Up Savings Apps:** Rounding up purchases to the nearest dollar when shopping online. Annual Savings: $300–$500, depending on your spending habits. If you're already a self-identified shopaholic, this may not be the best idea. Instead, try number 4.

4. **No-Spend Days:** One no-spend day per week, where you don't buy anything. There are also "Buy Nothing" groups on Facebook or in your local community where you can barter or trade for goods and services to support your no-spend days. Annual Savings: $520, assuming you save $10 on each no-spend day.

5. **Meal Planning:** Reduce costs for eating out by planning your meals ahead instead of getting fast food, takeout, or eating at restaurants. Annual Savings: $1,200, assuming you save $100 per month.

6. **Pack Lunches for Work:** Instead of buying lunch during your day, going to the vending machine, or getting delivery, bring your lunch from home. Annual Savings: $1,000, assuming you save at least $5 per day.

## Saving "F— You Money" for Financial Security

It probably won't take long for you to find big and small reasons to save. Whatever your savings goal, please let me give you one more: an F— You Money fund (FYM). FYM is any amount of money saved in a secure place that enables a person to walk away when it's time to go. You need FYM to get out of a situation, relationship, job, home, town, or environment without having to rely on anyone but yourself and your FYM stash. It doesn't necessarily have to be a bad situation, nor does your FYM fund have to replace all your income. It could be just enough money to allow you to prioritize yourself, right now, at this moment, to take advantage of an opportunity or to take some time off to figure things out. There is no set amount, because it depends solely on you and your lifestyle. The exciting thing about FYM is that in the beginning you may have saved up just enough to take a day off from work and not worry about lost wages when you really need a mental health day but are out of PTO. As you keep saving small amounts over time, you'll find your FYM growing big enough to float you for a couple of months, if you decide to move cross-country without having a new job lined up. And of course, FYM can be a lifesaver if you or a loved one are faced with an emergency and you need cash fast. Think through your needs and calculate how much you'll need so you can put yourself in a position to say F— YOU! Then start stashing your cash in small doses.

These days, knowing that I have a safety net that I can rely on to catch me during financial emergencies is incredibly important to me, as I know it is for most people. I want to emphasize that financial emergencies can take many forms and are unique to each individual's situation. While there are some emergency situations that are commonly recognized, there are also some that do not adhere to the conventional norm. Let me share a personal example. In 2021, I relocated six hundred miles away from my family to a town where I had very little community and friends. I anticipated the possibility of sudden family obligations arising and demanding my immediate presence back home. Rather than wait until something happened, I started saving money in small increments for "Emergency Travel." This money was separate from my vacation fund and could be used only in moments such as this. This scenario became a reality when my youngest son's grandmother passed away, propelling us into an abrupt trip from Atlanta to St. Louis. Despite our short time there—

flying in the evening before the funeral and leaving immediately after the service—the cost of plane tickets, hotel accommodations, and other related expenses would have put a strain on my finances and forced me to either dip into money saved for other expenses or use a credit card.

Despite the distance, the emotional connection and responsibility I felt to support my son made this situation a genuine emergency for me. Some may not believe that a situation happening six hundred miles away is an emergency, but my personal circumstances transformed this into one for me. This is why it is important for you to define what an emergency is to you and prepare for the potential risks specific to your circumstances.

I would define a financial emergency as any act or event that has the potential to put your financial stability at risk. That can be as common as a medical emergency or as unconventional as a canceled hair appointment. Defining what a financial emergency is for you means embracing the fact that they are not one-size-fits-all, and that you can prioritize saving for whatever is important to *you*.

## Breaking Down My Emergency Savings Strategy

You can call it a rainy-day fund like my mom, or FYM like me, or just plain old emergency savings. What's important to remember is that not all emergencies are created equal. Smartly managing an emergency fund is more about how you use the money than just saving it up. It's important to clearly define for yourself what counts as an emergency and then categorize your emergencies to avoid slowly depleting your funds by using your savings meant for big emergencies on minor inconveniences. To make sure I have enough money to cover the major financial hardships, I like to separate my emergency savings into specific categories and tiers based on the anticipated duration of the financial need and how long it will take to recover.

**Tier 1—Small Cash Emergencies (Immediate):** these are minor inconveniences less than $100, such as unexpected parking fees when visiting a new city or cash-only entry fees for fairs or sporting events.

**Tier 2—Short-Term Emergencies (1–3 months):** more costly but manageable onetime or short-term disruptions, such as minor home repairs (think broken window or leaking sink), or replacing devices or small appliances (a lost cell phone or ancient dishwasher).

**Tier 3—Medium-Term Emergencies (3–5 months):** significant financial hits that might take a few months to recover from, like major car repairs (transmission or engine) or unplanned travel expenses for a family emergency.

**Tier 4—Long-Term Emergencies (6+ months):** this category includes only severe, potentially life-altering financial hardships, such as recovering from a serious illness, sudden job loss, or natural disasters such as floods or fires impacting your home and living situation.

I handle these tiers for my family by creating four separate savings accounts. This keeps me from using money meant for serious emergencies on minor problems. This is what works for me, but if that feels overwhelming and you prefer using one account, that's fine. You may want to consider setting certain spending rules for yourself if you're pulling money from one big fund. For example, you can create percentages for each tier, allocating a certain amount for each category. You may budget 10 percent for Tier 1, 20 percent for Tier 2, 30 percent for Tier 3, and 40 percent for Tier 4 emergencies.

This doesn't mean you have to max out every single one of these tiers or accounts, but it's helpful to divide your emergency savings according to priorities. By doing so you ensure that each type of emergency has an appropriate safety net, preventing any single event from wiping out your entire emergency fund. By setting clear rules ahead of time, your emergency fund can support you when you truly need it.

## Incremental Saving Is a Superpower for Financial Security

The power of incremental saving doesn't lie only in its ability to protect you from financial emergencies. It also serves as the foundation for strategically saving for specific future expenses. In personal finance, you will often hear this method referred to as sinking funds. Sinking funds allow you to be proactive and set savings aside for a specific purpose and time frame, helping you prepare in advance for anticipated expenses and goals. My mom encouraged me to save because she knew the benefits of starting small and how my savings could grow over time, but there was no real plan for the money besides "saving for a rainy day." Sinking funds put a purpose behind your saving. With sinking funds, you have the option to create objectives for your money and break them down into tangible goals. It doesn't matter if it's something as large as the down payment for a house, a dream vacation, or something as small as concert tickets or a new pair of shoes.

Life has thrown a few challenges my way in the last couple decades that have taught me a valuable lesson about financial preparedness. It was during those times that I felt the weight of missed opportunities the most. We've all been there, looking back at our past selves and regretting having spent money we could have saved. Rather than succumbing to regret, I decided to finally take my mom's advice and realize that I still had time to make a difference. Sure, I may have missed out on some opportunities in the past, but it's always better late than never. Consider this perspective: Starting late comes with certain advantages. You now have the wisdom and experience to make informed decisions and avoid traps that tripped you up before. Yes, you may have missed out on a few opportunities, but that's the thing about in-cremental saving: it takes the pressure off saving money and makes it less of a race against the clock, because it's not about who's the fastest or who started the earliest. It's about consistency and progress, allowing you to set your own pace and focus on your journey rather than the destination.

Today, as a single mom of two teens, incremental saving is our family's superpower for achieving our big dreams. Every few months my sons and I sit down together and map out our dreams for the years. Then we look at the costs, break them down into small monthly savings actions, and get excited for what's to come. They know flying out to see family anytime it's needed is a priority for me, so that's an ongoing big dream for us. Our other big dreams look like: new football equipment in the fall (yes, they outgrow their gear every season), traveling once a year with their friends to celebrate their birthdays, saving for a small used car for my oldest son as he approaches driving age, and setting funds to the side for a big cross-country road trip we've been dreaming about for years. And I still love to spend money on hanging out with my friends. There will always be room for these things in our financial picture.

## Capable, Challenging, Creative

I still think about sixteen-year-old Dasha when folks ask me for help with building a financial safety net. That kid had a lot to learn, but like I said earlier, her kid-size money concerns were still valid. It doesn't matter why we're feeling stressed about money or what our financial priorities might be. If money feels tight, we'll resist saving because today's priorities will compete for our cash. The ironic thing is that the most important time to save *is when money feels tight*. Having that financial cushion will help ease the money stress. But it's also the hardest time to save—so something has to give, and usually, it's our mindset.

No matter how small a paycheck might be, if you can align your spending with your income, you can find something to save (yes, that's budgeting!). I've found that the key to saving is making sure you're **capable** of sustaining your plan, that it's **challenging** on some level, and that you get **creative** with how you save. Let me break that down a little more:

**Capable:** It would be nice to save $300 per month so you can fund a vacation in six months, but that's not realistic if it cuts into the cash you need to fund your basic needs. Yes, it's good to challenge yourself—more on this in a second—but don't sacrifice your well-being. You need to be capable of sustaining your savings plan.

**Challenging:** Incremental saving is all about balance. Don't save so hard that you're cutting off your basic needs, but at the same time, challenge yourself to get out of your comfort zone. This will be easier to do if you're sinking funds into something that means a lot to you. A vague emergency isn't motivating, but how about aiming to save $3,000 for when your house's twenty-year-old HVAC unit dies (and you know it will, likely during a record-breaking heat wave). Set your goal and then get a little ambitious with your incremental savings amount.

**Creative:** Sometimes you need to get creative to hit your savings goal, at least for a little while. If your current income truly doesn't allow you to save at a pace that can help you hit some goals, try increasing your income with a side hustle, even if it's temporary. Sell items on eBay or Facebook Marketplace, deliver food for Grubhub or Uber Eats, sell services in Fiverr, babysit, become a virtual assistant, walk dogs, clean houses. . . . There is so much that any of us can do to earn a little more if we need to. And I know that these are things you may hear all the time—trust me, I roll my eyes when I see them, too, but I want you to consider that none of these have to be long-term commitments—focus on the "little more" part. These can simply be stepping stones toward your financial goals, providing that extra bit of income when you need it most.

We can always find a good reason to quit saving—it starts to feel too difficult or too slow, or we lose motivation for our big dream. Keeping these three points at the center of your saving strategy will help keep it from getting stale.

## Weekly Savings Challenges: Dream Big, Think Small, in Action

Weekly challenges are my favorite way to hit a savings goal. Here's how they work: start with a small dollar amount, and then push yourself to save a little more each week. The most popular challenge among my online community is the $1,000 emergency fund challenge. We start by saving $1 a week, and every week we add a dollar to our savings amount. After fifty-two weeks you actually end up with $1,378. Here's what that looks like:

## 52-WEEK $1 SAVING CHALLENGE

Week 1, you save $1. In week 2, you save $2, which continues until week 52, adding one more dollar to each week's savings goal.

| | | | |
|---|---|---|---|
| Week 1: $1 | Week 14: $14 | Week 27: $27 | Week 40: $40 |
| Week 2: $2 | Week 15: $15 | Week 28: $28 | Week 41: $41 |
| Week 3: $3 | Week 16: $16 | Week 29: $29 | Week 42: $42 |
| Week 4: $4 | Week 17: $17 | Week 30: $30 | Week 43: $43 |
| Week 5: $5 | Week 18: $18 | Week 31: $31 | Week 44: $44 |
| Week 6: $6 | Week 19: $19 | Week 32: $32 | Week 45: $45 |
| Week 7: $7 | Week 20: $20 | Week 33: $33 | Week 46: $46 |
| Week 8: $8 | Week 21: $21 | Week 34: $34 | Week 47: $47 |
| Week 9: $9 | Week 22: $22 | Week 35: $35 | Week 48: $48 |
| Week 10: $10 | Week 23: $23 | Week 36: $36 | Week 49: $49 |
| Week 11: $11 | Week 24: $24 | Week 37: $37 | Week 50: $50 |
| Week 12: $12 | Week 25: $25 | Week 38: $38 | Week 51: $51 |
| Week 13: $13 | Week 26: $26 | Week 39: $39 | Week 52: $52 |
| | | | TOTAL SAVINGS |
| | | | $1,378 |

This is the power of dream big, think small in action. People always ask me why I don't suggest just splitting up the amount evenly across every week. In this case, that would be $26.50 a week, which is doable for many people. I prefer the incremental increases because it pushes you out of your comfort zone and gets you engaged with your finances. This isn't a set-it-and-forget-it savings approach. I recommend that, too, and that's when the same recurring amount makes sense since you're ideally doing automatic transfers to your savings account. But these challenges are a little extra. They're for a finite period of time and specifically for when you want to save more, faster.

Like I said earlier, this is the ultimate example of perseverance in personal finance. Many people feel they can't save and create a strong financial foundation for themselves. According to a YouGov survey for the Economic Security Project, 49 percent of US adults said they don't have the funds to cover a $400 emergency.[1] That means nearly half of US adults are one emergency away from a financial disaster. Everyone needs a financial security net, and everyone can have one. You may not be able to save up months' worth of expenses in one year—that's a recommended end goal, not the immediate goal—but you can work your way up there. I recommend finding a comfortable starting point, even if it's one month of expenses or half of your largest monthly bill. It's easier to come up with the remaining 50 percent of a bill than it is the full 100 percent of a bill when times are tough.

I love that these weekly challenges show us what's possible, and how saving money in small increments builds momentum. The reason why the popular "stop buying lattes" method does not work is because it encourages total and immediate deprivation of something you may enjoy that often leads to overconsumption. It also puts 100 percent of the blame on you for not being able to save money, when we know that not to be true for most people. The one thing the "latte method" does get correct is that saving small, consistent amounts can lead to a series of psychological and financial wins over time. Psychologically, just knowing that I was making progress toward my savings goals, no matter how slowly, reduced my stress and anxiety tremendously and instilled a sense of pride and confidence that I was doing all I could to take care of myself and my family. Financially, I felt a sense of empowerment and hope as I saw my savings grow incrementally, which motivated me to keep pushing toward additional goals like investing. It even became fun as I realized that saving added to my anticipation of holidays or va-

---

1 https://economicsecurityproject.org/news/economic-security-project-releases-yougov-public-opinion-research-signifying-striking-increase-in-americans-unable-to-cover-emergency-expenses-using-cash/.

cations, knowing that I was financially prepared instead of dreading these special occasions.

If you're not convinced yet, I challenge you to try out my $50 End of the Day Savings Challenge. I'm sure this quick win will help you experience the satisfaction of incremental savings in action.

## $50 End of the Day Savings Challenge

**Goal:** Reduce or eliminate expenses to save a total of $50 minimum before the end of today.

**How:** Reach out to all your service providers to discuss discounts, scaling back services, asking about more cost-effective plans, or canceling subscriptions you no longer use.

1 Call your cell phone provider to check for lower rates & deals.
2 Look over your subscriptions and cancel any you don't use.
3 Ask your insurance company about discounts you qualify for.
4 Speak with your bank about dropping any fees you're paying.
5 Check with utility providers for better rates or discounts.
6 Find a coupon or discount code for an upcoming large purchase.
7 Ask your creditors about hardship programs.

What can you do with that $50 you saved today?
- Quality-of-life purchases such as a monthly gym membership
- Strategic financial moves such as adding it to your investments, savings account, or debt reduction
- Financial security expenses such as covering a monthly life insurance premium

What can you do with $600 if you implement one $50 savings day a month (based on national averages for one person)?
- Buy six to ten extra weeks' worth of groceries
- Make an extra car payment

- Make two additional credit card payments
- Pay one and a half additional months' worth of utility bills
- Cover three to five year's gym membership
- Pay for nearly two years of life insurance
- Afford a year of streaming services
- Pay nine additional months of internet
- Cover about four additional months of a cell phone plan

Incremental savings allow you to dream big while thinking small and building your financial security one dollar at a time.

# CHAPTER 3

# Bank on Yourself (Banking)

When I picked up the phone, I could immediately tell my mom was angry by the way she said *Dasha!* with an urgency that made my blood go cold. I'd been at the mall all afternoon with my friends, shopping and spending the money I'd earned from my part-time job. My fun was canceled when Mom demanded I stop using my bank card *right now!* I understood she was upset, but I didn't fully grasp the gravity of the situation.

What had I done wrong? I'd been putting about $500 into our joint checking account every two weeks. Shouldn't I have been able to spend it how I wanted?

I was eighteen at the time and had no idea how debit cards, or bank accounts, worked. My mom had added me as an authorized user on her account so I could deposit paychecks from my retail job. I used a debit card connected to the account for shopping, and I thought it worked like cash in that once my money was spent, that would be it; my debit card would stop working. I didn't realize the bank wouldn't keep track of my deposits versus my mom's deposits and allow me to continue charging the card well beyond my $500. So, I just kept spending.

On the afternoon that my mom called, she'd received a notification from the bank alerting her that our joint account had been overdrawn. Not only had I spent all my money that month, but I'd also spent all her money in the account. I'd bought clothes and shoes with the money she'd put aside for unexpected expenses. Looking back now with the experience of being a single mother myself, I'm impressed my mom didn't completely lose it on me in that moment. I know the stress of having to stretch every dollar, and that even the slightest deviation from the plan could throw everything out of whack. It must have been disheartening to watch her hard-earned dollars drain out of the account with every swipe of my card. Thankfully, the joint account wasn't my mom's main expense account. However, it was holding a small emergency fund that she'd worked extremely hard to build up, so losing even the smallest amount directly impacted her sense of financial stability.

This was not a small inconvenience, although my error was completely innocent. On a deeper level, it illustrated issues with trust, communication, and the shared responsibility of managing our joint account. I wasn't paying attention or tracking my expenses, to my mom's detriment. This money wasn't easy or quick to replace, and my disregard for her very real concerns as our family's sole provider left our financial relationship strained.

Instead of guilt-tripping or punishing me for spending all her money, my mom just kicked me off our joint account and told me to get my own. It was her way of teaching me accountability. But there was one problem: at the time, I didn't know how to go about choosing the right financial institution for myself, let alone a bank account. That led to a lot of trouble until I figured out how banks work, and how to leverage them to support my financial goals.

**Payday loan offices are basically the same as banks, right?** *Wrong.*

I wanted to believe I could navigate banking on my own. I had every intention of opening a bank account, but the enticing neon signs of check-cashing and payday loan shops were everywhere on the south side of St. Louis. Their promises of quick cash and financial relief felt like a godsend in the face of the financial challenges I'd brought on myself by overdrawing my mom's account. Receiving cash up front and paying it back in small amounts seemed like a genius solution to my problems.

I was receiving paper paychecks at the time, not direct deposits as are common now. So, I would spend my thirty-minute lunch break racing across the parking lot to cash my paper check at a local check-cashing store or borrow one of my coworkers' cars to drive to another check-cashing store with "lower fees" a few blocks down the road. Yes, I did all that even though I happened to work directly across from a bank.

Looking back, I know I was naive to fall into their trap, but I also understand that the predatory practices of payday loans and check-cashing places were designed to trap me. Multiple studies have found that payday lenders and check-cashing stores are more likely to open in neighborhoods with predominantly Black or Hispanic populations.[1] They deliberately target people who may not have access to traditional banking services or don't know that banks provide more comprehensive offerings, lower interest rates, and opportunities for long-term financial stability. I had no idea back then, so I slid deeper and deeper into the vortex of short-term loans with high interest rates and fees that were intended to trick borrowers into a cycle of debt.

Check-cashing stores also caught my attention for a different reason. Aside from the promise of quick cash now, the fear of banks stealing my money or treating me unfairly was so deeply ingrained in my mind that I believed they were the better option. Yes, I'd relied on a bank when I used my mom's shared account, because it was convenient, yet my mistrust of banks always lingered in the background. I was inexperienced

---

1    https://libertystreeteconomics.newyorkfed.org/2012/02/do-payday-lenders-target-
     minorities/#:~:text=A%20number%20of%20studies%2C%20summarized,Hispanic%20
     and%2For%20black%20populations.

and trusted my mom with our joint account, but now that I was left on my own to manage my money, the warnings I'd heard about banks while growing up were ringing in my ears. I thought I was doing the right thing by staying away from them. It wasn't just that I didn't know any better—favoring check-cashing stores over banks was also based on having seen the effects of discriminatory banking practices firsthand.

**As a young Black woman, I had trust issues with banks for good reason.**

The historical context of mistrust and exploitation has shaped the relationship between the Black community and banks. Stories of lost savings, predatory lending practices, and unequal treatment have been passed down through generations, fueling skepticism of and caution toward mainstream financial institutions. My own family's experiences significantly influenced my perception of the financial industry, especially our personal history of being mistreated by banks over generations. I vividly remember my parents and family elders discussing that they were denied loans, charged extra fees because of low or no credit, and often felt unwelcome when visiting the bank. These stories left a lasting impression on me and made me doubt that banks had our best interests at heart.

After the Civil War, Freedman's Savings Bank was established to help previously enslaved people access financial services. Due to mismanagement and fraud, such as bank trustees investing in risky real estate projects and giving loans to friends without collateral, the bank collapsed in 1874. Many historians believe that Freedman's Bank losing the savings of tens of thousands of Black customers created a deep distrust of financial institutions in the Black community that still lingers today.[2]

Similar practices continued over generations. In the mid-twentieth century, a practice known as contract buying became widespread, especially in Chicago. Black families were barred from regular mort-

---

2    https://home.treasury.gov/about/history/freedmans-bank-building/freedmans-bank-demise#:~:text=When%20a%20financial%20panic%20hit,of%20depositors%20demanded%20their%20money._

gages and forced into land sale contracts that were heavily skewed in favor of sellers and lenders. These contracts imposed high interest rates and could result in foreclosure if a single payment was missed.

Around the same time, the financial sector instituted "redlining"— withholding services from residents living in "high-risk" areas that just happened to be primarily Black neighborhoods.[3] My grandparents, especially my grandmothers, recounted personal experiences of redlining and being denied mortgages in certain neighborhoods solely because of their race. Because of these systemic inequities, my great-grandmother was the only homeowner in my family for decades. Four generations lived in her house at the same time and told these stories at family gatherings as a constant reminder to me that banks were not to be trusted.

In the 2000s, Wells Fargo faced allegations from the Department of Justice that steered African American and Hispanic borrowers into subprime loans or charged them higher fees compared to non-Hispanic white borrowers with similar credit profiles. These practices were said to have contributed to higher foreclosure risks for affected borrowers. Wells Fargo ultimately reached a settlement with the Department of Justice to avoid contested litigation, agreeing to pay close to $200 million in relief to impacted borrowers.[4]

While I wasn't familiar with all this history as a teen, I felt a general sense of unease toward banks since I'd grown up hearing those family stories. And I wasn't alone. A 2023 survey showed that distrust in banks was the second-most-cited reason for individuals without a bank account, right after not being able to meet the minimum balance

---

3    Beryl Satter, *Family Properties: Race, Real Estate, and the Exploitation of Black Urban America* (New York: Metropolitan Books, 2009).

4    https://www.justice.gov/opa/pr/justice-department-reaches-settlement-wells-fargo-resulting-more-175-million-relief.

requirement.[5] Looking back, it's clear that payday loans and check-cashing places were only the newest attempt in a long line of exploitative practices to prevent Black Americans from building wealth. Just like me, many of my friends and family members resorted to these alternative financial services despite their high costs and risks. Once the cash was in your hands, the deal was done, and the risk of having your money stolen or mishandled was gone. It's a vicious and seemingly never-ending cycle where the Black community often ends up paying more for financial services.

After "Joint-Account-Gate," I was embarrassed to confess my dire situation to my mom but eventually realized that I needed help. Thankfully, she didn't leave me to fend for myself. Despite her frustration, she understood the importance of teaching me how to manage a bank account. My mom was young when she had me and didn't regularly use banks up until a few years before I was old enough to get my own account. In many ways, we learned together, my mom just a few steps ahead of me in the process. She didn't judge me, but instead encouraged me again to get my own account at an actual bank. This time, she made sure to remind me there would be no backup plan or extra money in the account because I was now solely responsible for all my financial decisions.

Opening my first bank account when I turned eighteen was a revolutionary act. Hear me out.

Women couldn't open a bank account in their own name until the 1960s, and many banks still required a signature from their husbands. This resulted in single women regularly being refused banking services altogether, while married women depended on their husbands' permission.[6] Even after the Equal Credit Opportunity Act in 1974

---

5    https://www.fdic.gov/analysis/household-survey/index.html.

6    https://www.forbes.com/advisor/banking/when-could-women-open-a-bank-account
/#:~:text=It%20wasn't%20until%201974,a%20signature%20from%20their%20husbands.

prohibited banks from discriminating against applicants based on sex, marital status, and race,[7] women continued to face significant barriers to financial services like lines of credit and loans due to lingering biases and stereotypes.

Today, women are still one of the largest underserved and underrepresented groups when it comes to financial services,[8] yet women make more than 80 percent of the banking decisions for their families.[9] Access to financial services acts as a gateway to economic opportunities. Despite the tireless work of Black women in finance who have carved out a space for me within these institutions, there is still much work to be done.

Despite the fact that more banks have made efforts to improve their services and practices, and customers have more access to objective information about their bank, it remains challenging to break away from the cycle of mistrust—especially for older generations. My grandparents and great-grandparents grew up in a time when financial discrimination was widespread, and my mother's generation is the first to see a slow change happening. I don't think my mom had the historical significance of a bank account for a young Black woman in mind when she kicked me off her account. She was just frustrated that my reckless spending was causing her financial harm. But she made up for it when she helped me get back on my feet by opening my own bank account.

So I'm not exaggerating when I say that every time a young Black woman opens a bank account, she becomes part of a larger movement—a refusal to let our financial well-being be determined by societal limitations. It's a symbol of resistance and resilience, an act of self-empowerment, and a declaration to the world that we are the architects of our financial futures.

---

7    https://prologue.blogs.archives.gov/2023/03/22/on-the-basis-of-sex-equal-credit-opportunities/.

8    https://www.fdic.gov/analysis/household-survey/index.html.

9    https://www.bankrate.com/loans/personal-loans/purchasing-power-of-women-statistics/#purchasing.

To me, my mom embodied this symbol of resistance and resilience when she set a crucial example for me, against all odds, by opening a bank account and helping me do the same.

## Let's Be the Change, and Do It with Confidence

As empowering as opening a bank account can be, it can also be extremely confusing. There are so many financial institutions to choose from, so many different kinds of accounts, and endless fine print that may or may not be a big deal. I often hear from folks who feel so intimidated by all the choices and financial jargon, it keeps them from opening any bank account at all. Then, once you have an account, there's the lingering question of whether you're using it to its fullest potential, or whether another option would serve you better.

It's tempting to dismiss the banking conversation as basic. In fact, most personal finance advice overlooks it completely and focuses solely on topics like budgeting, saving, and investing. But that's a big oversight. Yes, talking about bank accounts can feel as basic as ordering a pumpkin spice latte at the coffee shop on September 1, but walk with me on this: where you bank is central to your wealth-building ambitions. You've got to get this right.

Opening a bank account is one of the most important steps in your financial journey. I'm going to take the mystery out of the process so you can make smart choices without feeling lost or doubting yourself. And I'll start with a question that most people who are new to money management may not even realize they should be asking. . . .

### What Exactly *Is* a Bank?

I know, right? I wish someone had explained this to me when I was just starting out. A bank is a financial institution that acts as a safe place for you to deposit and grow your money, and it frequently offers other financial products, such as loans and credit lines. Banks make most of their money by using a part of the funds their customers deposit into checking and savings accounts as capital to grant loans to individuals and businesses. The interest they charge for these loans is how they make a profit. Banks also make money from charging customers a variety of fees, such as ATM, late, or overdraft fees, loan origination fees, or fees for asset management and investments.

Reliable banks are insured by the Federal Deposit Insurance Corporation (FDIC), an independent agency created by Congress to maintain stability and public confidence in the US financial system in 1933. The FDIC provides deposit insurance for your funds up to $250,000 in the event of a bank collapse. In other words, the FDIC pays you up to $250,000 of your account balance, even if your bank shuts down. If FDIC insurance had been established at the time Freedman's Bank collapsed, those Black families would not have lost all their savings.

Banks play a major role in our economy by facilitating the flow of money and providing essential financial services. They serve as a go-between between people who have excess money (depositors) and those who need to borrow money (borrowers). This is a long way from keeping cash under the mattress or in a shoebox in the closet.

Banks typically offer checking and savings accounts and loan products such as home mortgages, car loans, and personal loans to finance major purchases or cover emergency expenses.

I'm often asked how bank loans differ from payday loans, which is an important question. Payday loans are easy and quick to apply for, but they need to be repaid by your next payday, charge high interest rates, and have hidden fees. Bank loans generally have much lower interest rates and give you more time to pay them back, while requiring a more complex application. Dealing with the annoyance of a longer application is well worth it, because one of the main reasons is to determine your ability to pay back the loan, making it less risky for both you and the bank to enter into an agreement. The less risk, the less it costs. The average payday loan charges 400 percent interest,[10] while the average personal loan from a bank offers interest rates between 5 percent and 36 percent.[11]

The bank takes into consideration how much money you make, how much debt you already have, and how reliably you've paid other loans back in the past. This information determines how much money the bank will lend you, the interest rate, and how much time you'll have to repay the loan. Bank loan interest rates and terms vary depending on the amount you borrow, your credit history and score, and competitors' rates. The federal funds rate is set by the Federal Reserve and dictates how much it costs for banks to borrow money from other banks, which impacts how much the bank will charge you to borrow money from them. Because the federal funds rate is the same for all US banks, it makes the interest rates for your personal loan more stable and competitive.

All these banking regulations help keep the playing field fairly even and make banks a safer, more stable option for accessing financial services and borrowing money than payday loans and check-cashing places. However, there are some important differences in the fine print when comparing banks to each other, and that's where it can get a bit tricky. Banks differ in size, structure, and service offerings. In your community, you'll likely have the option to choose between local or regional banks and credit unions, and large national or even international institutions.

Credit unions are hyperlocal. They're your actual neighbors, serving as financial institutions for your community or region. While banks are for-profit companies, credit unions are not for profit and distribute their profits among members. They don't offer as many services as giant national bank chains, but they have a human touch, in addition to offering lower interest and reduced fees. And because they're local,

---

10   Consumer Federation of America (CFA): https://paydayloaninfo.org/how-payday-loans-work/

11   *Forbes:* https://www.forbes.com/advisor/personal-loans/personal-loan-rates/.

they're much more invested in the community and in helping you out as their customer.

When I applied to get a car loan, I was denied by several banks, including the one I worked for. After they reviewed my application, I was also denied initially by a credit union. However, a customer representative called me a day later, asked more questions about my employment, my need for the loan, and how much I could afford to pay every month. After the conversation, the credit union overturned the denial and approved me to purchase my first car.

Credit unions, with their community-oriented approach, are often more willing to consider individual circumstances, take the time to understand a member's financial needs, and work toward finding solutions. With larger banks, the decision-making process can sometimes feel impersonal and heavily reliant on strict criteria. However, they also offer the largest variety of services and bank accounts. Sometimes, smaller, regional banks can provide the sweet spot you're looking for, but it's all about your personal preferences.

Before you dig into the process of choosing a financial institution, it helps to know what kind of account you need and then work from there. That way, you can vet each place based first on whether they have what you're looking for, and then on the details of what they offer for the type of account you need.

### Choosing the Right Type of Account to Meet Your Needs and Goals

The first question to ask yourself before opening a bank account is: "Why do I need this account, and how will I use it?" Even if you've already opened an account, it's still important to take a step back to consider your financial needs and goals. Most people primarily need a bank account for direct deposits of wages or salary.

In this case, a basic checking account to manage your everyday expenses might be all you need. But how about a savings account with a competitive interest rate to grow your money and set it aside for future goals or emergencies? That's what I should have opened when my mom suggested I put away $20 a month, and I eventually did. Looking beyond checking and savings accounts, as your savings grows you may eventually be interested in other financial products for investing, growing your business, or buying a home.

Let's dig into the details of the types of accounts available to fit your financial goals.

## Checking Accounts

This is the most basic account nearly everyone will get the most use out of for day-to-day transactions. A checking account allows you to deposit your income, pay bills, withdraw cash, and access your funds through various channels like debit cards, checks, and digital transfers. As you're just starting out, it helps to look for a checking account that offers low or no monthly maintenance fees and no minimum balance.

Most checking accounts come with a debit card that is directly linked to your account. When you make a purchase using that card, the money is immediately deducted from your account balance. As I learned the hard way, though, depending on your bank's overdraft protection rules, you may be able to make purchases with your debit card after your money has run out, putting you in the negative. This will depend on whether your account has overdraft protection, and the terms of that protection. Also pay attention to details like your debit card's daily transaction limits, ATM access and fees, and fraud protection. I'll go into more detail on each of these later in this chapter.

## Savings Accounts

Savings accounts are a safe place to store your money over longer periods of time while earning interest on your account balance. They can provide a buffer for emergency expenses and help you work toward savings goals like taking your kids on a beach vacation or replacing your ancient laptop. They often require a minimum balance at all times, which is one of the main differences from a checking account, aside from offering higher interest rates.

High-yield savings accounts are a subtype typically offered by online-only banks that operate with lower overhead costs, allowing them to pass on better interest rates to their customers. They're an excellent option to earn more on your savings balance, if access to a local branch isn't important to you.

Look for a savings account with competitive interest rates, low minimum-balance requirements, and low or no monthly maintenance fees.

Now, to be clear, you don't *need* to have a savings account to save money. You can save in your checking account. But having a separate account for your savings often helps on a practical level, and with your mindset. For one thing, you can't access those funds with your debit card, so they're safe from impulse buys or any fraudulent activity on your card. There's also something to be said for keeping your savings separate from the account that you do your daily spending and bill paying from. It earmarks that money for something beyond everyday expenses and offers a sense of financial security. Savings accounts also typically offer higher interest rates than checking accounts, which helps your money grow while it sits there—even if it's just a little.

## Money Market Accounts

This hybrid account blends features of both checking and savings accounts. Money market accounts typically offer higher interest rates than regular savings accounts while also providing limited check-writing abilities to access funds. These accounts strike a balance between earning potential and maintaining some fund liquidity.

Here's a quick overview comparing the advantages and disadvantages of each account type so you can make an informed choice.

| Account Type | Advantages | Disadvantages | Common Uses |
|---|---|---|---|
| *Checking* | Easy access to funds<br><br>No limits on number of transactions<br><br>Usually no balance requirements<br><br>Often comes with debit cards and checks<br><br>Access to online banking services | Typically low or no interest on account balances<br><br>Might have dollar-value transaction limits<br><br>Can be easier to overspend with overdraft protection | Daily use for depositing income<br><br>Bill pay<br><br>Debit card purchases |
| *Savings* | Earns interest<br><br>Separates dedicated funds for long-term goals | No access to funds using checks or a debit card<br><br>Minimum-balance requirements | Dedicated fund for bigger expenses, emergencies, and long-term goals |
| *Money Market* | Often earns higher interest rates than regular savings accounts<br><br>May come with debit cards and checks | Only limited check-writing abilities<br><br>Interest rates may be lower than other longer-term investment options | Often used for daily transactions or savings since it combines features of checking accounts with higher interest rates of savings account |

## Speed-Dating Banks to Find Your Financial Soulmate

Now that you have an idea of what type of account(s) you might need, let's figure out what type of financial institution is the right match for you. Remember, you can change banks at any time, so there's no pressure to make the perfect decision. Even if you already have a bank, this exercise may help you realize that your current bank or accounts are not aligned with your goals. Maybe you've never taken the time to think about the expectations you have of your bank or weren't aware you could even have expectations in the first place.

Let's look at starting a banking relationship like any other relationship. Both parties are auditioning for each other to see if it's a match. Both sides get to have needs and expectations. You have to watch out for red flags and be clear on your deal-breakers. Sometimes you'll be compatible, and sometimes you won't. Maybe the first bank you try out won't be your type, after all. That's okay, dump them and move on!

It's crucial to set clear expectations up front so you can be sure that your banking experience meets your needs, reducing the risk of any unwanted "surprises" down the line. Let's walk through some of the qualities to consider when picking your perfect match:

## Style

Some of your needs and expectations from a bank may be tied to the way you like to do business. Do you prefer walking into a local branch to work with someone face-to-face, or are you the online-banking-from-the-couch-in-your-stretchy-pants type? Maybe you're both—and you can have it both ways with major banks that have a large physical presence paired with strong online tools. It's totally normal to try on different banks like outfits to see what feels comfortable and matches your style and personality. Don't let anyone rush you. Take your time to research and experiment.

Most traditional banks do have brick-and-mortar locations, so you can visit and sit down with tellers, loan officers, personal bankers, and branch managers to discuss what you're looking for in your perfect fit.

Most institutions also offer online banking services 24/7, allowing you to check balances, manage your budget, pay bills, transfer money between accounts, and deposit checks by taking a picture with your phone camera. These features are usually accessible through the bank's website and on their mobile app. You can bank from home, on the go, and on any device with an internet connection. There are plenty of online-only bank options, but most will be a hybrid, offering physical locations paired with online banking services.

## Online Banking Features

I use online banking features for financial management and planning. Some of the most common and useful tools include:

**Account management** shows me account balances in real time and allows me to review transaction history, including deposits, withdrawals, and purchases. I can make transfers between accounts and access monthly digital bank statements.

**Electronic bill pay** allows me to set up and manage my recurring bills, such as utilities, rent, and credit card payments. Automatic bill pay keeps track of due dates, which prevents late fees and saves time every month after the initial setup.

**Mobile banking apps** enable mobile deposits of checks using smartphone cameras, contactless payments with mobile wallets, and alerts in case of suspicious account activity, low balances, or missed payments.

**Budgeting tools** help me with expense tracking, saving, and goal setting. Aside from tracking account balances, I gain a better understanding of my spending habits over time, set savings goals, and monitor my progress. These tools categorize expenses and display them in a pie graph, so I always have a quick visual. This makes it hard to ignore that I spend ridiculous amounts of money on late-night Target runs.

Instead of having to track expenses manually and wasting a bunch of time working with incomplete and old data, my bank pulls accurate real-time information and does the math for me. My bank has become my accountability partner with these tools, immediately alerting me to red flags in my spending behavior.

**Investment management** enables online trading of stocks and bonds, viewing your investment portfolio and performance, and access to virtual financial advisers for basic investment information.

## Security

Whether you choose a traditional, online, or hybrid bank, pay close attention to their security measures protecting both your personal information and your money. In addition to ensuring your funds are protected by banking with an FDIC member institution, look for features such as encrypted online banking, multifactor authentication, and fraud monitoring systems. Different banks offer different layers of security. Consider a bank's history and track record. Have they been transparent with their customers about security issues in the past? Have they shown a commitment to improve security after a breach? With cybercrime and hackers growing more sophisticated, perfect security is becoming less and less realistic. However, the institution of your choice should be committed to improvement and being on top of the newest security issues and exploits.

## Fees and Charges

I look for the best deal when I go grocery shopping. Evaluating bank fees and charges is no different. Buying the store brand option for a few bucks cheaper than the brand name doesn't make much of a difference in a single trip to the store, but it adds up over months and years. It's the same with considering the fee structures of each bank, such as maintenance, overdraft, and ATM fees.

Some banks offer fee waivers under certain circumstances, or as perks for fulfilling particular requirements, such as keeping minimum account balances or just being a valued customer. They may waive fees for wire transfers or using cashier's checks. Getting clear on the fees associated with maintaining your bank account is a crucial deciding factor. These are some of the main fees to look out for.

**Maintenance Fees:** When I first opened my bank account, I struggled with the monthly maintenance fee. While it was only $5 a month, I didn't immediately consider and track it as an expense, which led me to overdraw my account regularly. Some banks waive these fees if you maintain a minimum balance or set up direct deposits.

**Overdraft Protection:** Many banks offer overdraft protection programs as a safety net, which is why Joint-Account-Gate didn't turn out as disastrous as it could have. These programs link your checking account to a savings account or line of credit. If you make a transaction that exceeds your account balance, the bank will automatically transfer funds to cover the overdraft. This can save you from hefty overdraft fees and declined transactions, but not the wrath of your mother.

You can opt out of overdraft protection, resulting in the bank declining any transaction that exceeds your available balance. While this may seem restrictive or lead to embarrassment in the checkout lane, it can be extremely helpful if you want to avoid temptations to overspend, but it comes with a fee.

Not all banks use the term "overdraft protection" the same way, so you need to find out what they consider the default (cover or decline overdrafts) and how you can opt out if necessary.

**ATM Fees:** After relocating to a new city, I didn't want to change one of my primary banks, even though there was no branch office near me for miles. I'd often have to use ATMs unrelated to my banks, which charged me higher fees. It may sound insignificant, but those charges add up, so I appreciate that my bank reimburses ATM fees. Look for banks that offer transparent fee policies or even fee-free options to avoid unnecessary costs.

## Special Perks

Banks compete for customers just like every other business, which often results in great perks for you to take advantage of, including rewards programs, discounts and partnerships, and financial education resources.

**Rewards Programs:** Some banks offer rewards programs tied to their debit or credit cards, so you can earn points or cashback on your purchases (we'll talk about credit cards in detail in chapter 8). If you're interested in playing the points game to redeem them for products or travel, this may be a deciding factor for you. Keep an eye out for banks that offer rewards aligned with your spending habits and preferences.

**Discounts and Partnerships:** Banks often partner with retailers and service providers to offer exclusive deals or discounts to customers, including travel, shopping, dining, and entertainment. Again, it matters most if the bank partners with brands you're already using or have a genuine interest in trying out. No point in choosing a bank for their free Hulu subscription when you're a Netflix type of girl.

**Financial Education Resources:** Many banks offer educational resources to improve financial literacy, covering everything from budgeting, saving, investing, and credit management and recovery. They may hold in-person workshops or offer online webinars, video tutorials, or articles. They may also share information on how to access specific specialized financial services they provide.

**Specialized Services:** Your financial institution likely has areas of specialized focus and expertise, such as programs for first-time homebuyers, small business banking solutions, or assistance for customers facing financial hardships. If you want to buy your first house or are starting a business, why not choose a bank that can provide expert support?

## Reputation

This is one situation where it's a good idea to pay attention to the he said/she said. Word of mouth and customer feedback online, such as ratings and reviews, are the primary ways you'll learn about a bank's reputation. Every bank has its pros and cons, so a few bad reviews aren't anything to worry about. Even the best restaurant will have a few diners who can't be pleased no matter what and complain that they wanted Mexican food even though they chose an Italian restaurant.

It's more important to pay attention to patterns in negative reviews, problems that come up repeatedly, like rude staff, glitchy online banking services, or hidden fees. Worried about any shady business or concerned a specific bank might not protect your money? Remember to check for FDIC insurance so you're covered no matter what happens to your bank.

A solid reputation will be reflected in overall above-average ratings and reviews. That doesn't mean it's the right bank for you, if it doesn't offer the services and products you need. That's why I suggest looking for banks that align with your goals and needs first and then ranking that list of options based on reputation.

## Time to Find Out If You Have Chemistry!

Once you've narrowed down your options for banks to a short list of about three to five, it's time you get to know each other. Visit the bank's branch or contact their customer service to get all your questions answered. You'll need firsthand experience to help you determine if you're comfortable with how the bank interacts with you as a prospective customer.

I worked in banking for a few years, and one of the most important lessons I learned early on is that customer service representatives are the face of the company. Are they professional, knowledgeable, and happy to answer your questions about products and features? Do they treat you, other customers, and coworkers in a friendly manner? Welcoming staff is a good indicator of a well-managed bank. If you're interacting with an online-only bank, try several different channels, such as phone calls, instant messaging on their website, or email. Make sure you feel well taken care of even without the face-to-face interaction of an in-person visit.

If the bank's staff are rude, dismissive, or unable to answer your questions, it's reasonable to conclude they won't be much help if you ever need to discuss fraudulent activity on your account or are trying to get back into your online banking platform after being locked out. These are red flags. Don't think they'll change once you've made a commitment to each other. You deserve better.

## Should It Matter to Your Bank That You're a Woman?

Absolutely. We need to put our money in a place that understands and empowers us.

Historically, the banking industry has taken a male-centric approach to its featured products and services, overlooking the unique needs and challenges faced by women. Women may have different financial goals, different income patterns, and family dynamics. I want to do business with innovative and progressive banks that offer services tailored to my needs and make me feel seen and heard.

I've lived in the inner city most of my life, and I remember only one occasion when a mainstream financial institution came to our community offering financial empowerment through education. The bank that earns my business not only shows up consistently to educate our community but specifically empowers women to make informed financial decisions through workshops, seminars, and specialized services. This is how banks contribute to closing the gender wealth gap.

A bank that deserves my business values diversity, progressive initiatives, and inclusivity in their decision-making progress, because they understand that diverse perspectives lead to better outcomes and more inclusive financial products.

In practice, this means the bank has racial, gender, and ethnic diversity at all levels, instead of just employing token minority staff in junior positions. Does the bank have a history of hiring and promoting women, people of color, immigrants, or neurodivergent individuals to leadership positions? Who makes the decisions at this institution, and who is involved in those processes? Are their buildings accessible to individuals who are differently abled physically? Are their services accessible to customers with English as their second language? By banking only with institutions that show up for women and minorities in real and practical ways, we can actively participate in shaping the future of financial services.

Some banks may actively share this information on their website, but more likely, you'll have to specifically ask for it when you interview banks during your search for the perfect fit.

## Checklist—What to Ask When Speed-Dating Banks

Here's a cheat sheet of questions to keep in mind as you're considering the right bank for you.

### ACCOUNTS AND FEATURES

- What type of accounts are available to me, and what are their associated costs and features?
- What are your interest rates, minimum-balance requirements, transaction limits, and overdraft protection policies for these types of accounts?
- What is your bank's ATM availability in this area, associated fees, and/or policy on fee reimbursement?
- Do you offer online banking, and if so, what are the main features?

### SECURITY AND SUPPORT

- Which customer service option do you offer (chat, email, phone, in person), and during which hours?
- What security measures do you have in place to protect my accounts and personal information?
- How does your bank ensure that banking services and education are accessible to individuals with disabilities?
- Are your services and resources available in different languages to cater to non–English speaking clients?

## RESOURCES AND EDUCATION

- Do you offer workshops, webinars, or seminars on financial literacy, and do they cater to the unique needs of different demographics?
- What kind of support, resources, or programs does your bank offer for small businesses, particularly those owned by women or individuals from minority communities?
- How does your bank support customers who are undergoing financial crises or hardships?

## INCLUSIVE COMMUNITY INITIATIVES

- How does your bank invest in local communities, especially underserved or marginalized groups lacking access to financial services?
- What practices does your bank have in place to promote social and environmental sustainability and ethics?
- What policies do you have in place to ensure representation of women and people of color within the bank's leadership and staff?

# CHAPTER 4

# Stuck with Student Loans
# (Education)

'I've dropped out of college four times. Each time I went back, I took out more student loans. Eventually, my student loan debt totaled about $20,000, and I still have about $5,000 left to pay. While it may not seem like a significant amount to some, it represented a major financial burden for me over the year. I took on this debt to earn a degree I thought would translate into dollars, better job opportunities, and economic power. I never completed my degree and haven't been able to leverage all that education in any direct way to increase my income in a traditional sense.

I had no idea what I was getting myself into with student loans. I was clueless about the terms, interest rate, repayment plan, or far-reaching consequences of taking on that debt. All I knew was that everywhere I turned, people pushed the idea of getting a college degree to advance my career, and I didn't have the financial means to pay for it out of pocket. I was too afraid to ask questions about the loans I was applying for because I didn't want to appear ignorant. Ironically, I worked with senior-level accountants who could have easily helped me, but I couldn't fathom asking them anything that would make me look uninformed. This fear resulted in a lack of knowledge and, eventually, a cycle of unnecessary debt I was struggling to repay.

Over the last fifteen years, I've tried to pay down my student loans without depleting a large portion of my monthly income. It was one of the biggest challenges on my journey to taking control of my finances, and I know I'm not alone. According to the National Center for Education Statistics, Black women have been obtaining degrees consistently for the last decade.[1] This supports a solid commitment to dedicating our time, money, and resources to pursuing higher education, as we've always been told was the right thing to do to move ahead. Yet even with comparable education, Black women still face challenges converting their degrees into dollars. So how in the hell are we supposed to get rid of student loan debt?

Making informed decisions about how educational expenses fit into your budget and wealth-building efforts is crucial. This is true whether you're considering going to college, are currently attending classes, or are already out of school and juggling student loans. The weight of educational expenses is especially heavy for women, who hold almost two-thirds of the total outstanding student loan debt balance.[2] Black women in particular have the highest student loan debt of any racial or ethnic group[3] and are more likely than other groups to take on student loan debt due to systemic disparities and limited access to financial resources.

Even with a degree, Black women face gender and race wage gaps. We earn much less than men and white women, making it even more

---

1   https://nces.ed.gov/fastfacts/display.asp?id=72.

2   https://www.aauw.org/resources/research/deeper-in-debt/.

3   https://www.aauw.org/resources/research/deeper-in-debt/.

difficult to manage student loan debt. African American student borrowers owe the highest monthly payments toward student loan debt compared to other ethnic groups, and 50 percent of Black student borrowers report their net worth is less than they owe in student loan debt.[4]

Put another way, low-income students, women, and especially Black women have been doing the work to complete higher education without receiving the promised benefits. Instead, we're left with piles of debt and a lack of funds for building wealth.

We can't talk about wealth building without shining a light on the price of higher education. Many of us have been taught that it's worth pursuing a college degree at any cost because it will eventually lead to greater financial security. Often, that's simply not true. Some of us learned this the hard way and are stuck paying loans for degrees we'll never use. But as I discovered, we're not as stuck as we may think. If you're early in your career and trying to figure out how you'll pay for your education, you also have more options than you may realize.

A college degree is not the ultimate ticket to financial security. Student loans are not the only path to a college degree. And putting a strain on your monthly cash flow to make student loan payments is not the only answer to paying off your debt. We have options—and the first step, if you're just starting out, is to figure out whether you need a college degree at all.

## Do Your Career Aspirations Even Require a College Degree?

I understand that many of you reading this book will be beyond the point of being able to make this choice. There's a good chance you already have student loans and are figuring out how to manage them.

---

4    https://educationdata.org/student-loan-debt-by-race.

But if you haven't pursued higher education yet and are exploring your options, please consider whether you need a degree at all.

I believe in the transformative power of higher education. It's just important to approach it strategically. If you have an idea of the career path you want to take, consider whether a traditional four-year college is the only way to get you there. Think about the types of jobs that interest you and whether college or trade school would help you advance in those careers. If you want to be a doctor, you will need an advanced medical degree. But if you want to be a jewelry designer, a metalsmithing course at a trade school or community college might do. I regret not narrowing down exactly what I wanted to do with my life prior to attending college. Not because I regret my experience but because I would have been able to make a more informed decision had I spent time figuring out my big-picture goals. It's key to align your educational path with your desired profession.

Most of us go to college with the idea that the money we spend will have some return on investment and result in higher-paying careers down the road. If I had a do-over, I'd first research the job market associated with the field I wanted to study so I could better understand the demand for my future skills and the kind of salary ranges to expect. In short, would I be able to get a job quickly and make enough money to offset the cost of my education?

Education is a complex issue. College offers a space for self-discovery and exploration, potentially leading you to find a career path you hadn't previously considered. But the same can happen when you enter the workforce and gain practical experience to guide your career trajectory. It's crucial to approach college with some intentionality, considering the significant financial investment. It's just as important to pay attention to continuing education opportunities while employed. In short, be strategic about your educational opportunities. Without a plan, there's a higher risk of financial loss due to accumulating student loan debt like I did in my four attempts, extended time in school, delaying your entry into the job market, or missing out on employer-sponsored educational options. Making decisions that align with your personal values and goals is essential, even if your initial plan isn't fully defined.

Whether or not we're aware of all the educational options available to us, the harsh reality for Black women is that often our degrees will end up on the shelf, collecting dust. Meanwhile, we're being crushed under the burden of student loan debt we expected to pay back easily with all those high-paying jobs we were promised and never got. That's a heavy mental and financial load to carry while we're also the primary caretakers for our kids and extended families.

## Does Higher Education Fit into Your Current Stage of Life?

I believed that a college education was the one thing missing from my life, and that I couldn't move up in my career without it. But every one of my college attempts had me struggling to overcome different barriers spanning logistics, transportation, finances, and childcare.

I excelled in writing and literature in high school and wanted to pursue a degree in journalism, so I started community college after taking a year off following my high school graduation. I went through the entire enrollment process, only to drop out a few months into classes because of persistent transportation issues. I didn't have a car then and relied on public transportation or rides from my family and friends. Getting back and forth to work and school on time was nearly impossible.

A few years later, I was introduced to a new option to attend college: online universities. It seemed like the perfect solution for a single mother like me who wanted to continue pursuing journalism while being able to take care of my baby boy from the comfort of my home. Well, not so much. Unfortunately, the fees for attending online school were much more expensive than my community college classes. On top of that, it was difficult to juggle being both a student and a mother in my small apartment. I couldn't find the balance and found myself falling behind before I even had the chance to get ahead.

Another few years went by before one of my coworkers told me about a night school program offered by a top college in my state. The counselor convinced me that I could attend school one night per week in an accelerated program and graduate within three to four years. One night per week? In-person classes? Right up the street from my job? Perfect! Unfortunately, this excitement was short-lived, since I was a recently divorced, single mother of two. That one extra night every week was enough to increase the number of day care hours beyond what I could afford in monthly childcare costs on my newly reduced income. Enrolling in an accelerated program for one night a week should have been the best option for me to pursue my degree in journalism and economic policy, but it didn't work out that way.

It's a tough choice to make. Do we continue pursuing our education, hoping for better opportunities in the long run, but risk financial strain and potentially falling into debt for that education? Or do we prioritize immediate financial stability and put our educational aspirations on hold, sacrificing the potential benefits?

I know now that it's okay to change my educational and career path if it's not financially feasible or doesn't align with my goals anymore. I eventually found my path in the finance industry, without a college degree. I've built a profitable career while positively impacting other people's lives, and I've advocated for economic justice and financial literacy for as long as I can remember.

I've now reached a point where I believe that furthering my education can amplify my ability to make a difference. I want to pursue degrees in law and agricultural economics because I see these fields as essential to the impact I want to have on my community. It will offer me the opportunity to address fundamental issues like food insecurity, land use, and sustainable farming practices, which all play a major part in a community's financial stability.

In the past, my lack of funds and the high cost of tuition forced me to drop out of school multiple times, while I was constantly juggling my work and childcare responsibilities. At this stage in my life, I can refocus on my education and go back to school without existential financial worries. All my previous detours have brought me to this point when I've figured out which degrees I want to pursue and have created the financial security I need to make it happen, so I can more effectively advocate for policy changes that rectify historical injustices.

## If You Do Need a College Degree, Know Your Options for Financing It

College in America is expensive AF. There's no way around it, and just like so many others, I had to rely on loans to cover the high cost of education.

When I first started thinking about college, the only options that were presented to me as an eighteen-year-old were student loans. I don't recall having a single conversation about financial aid or scholarships. Many organizations offer scholarships, especially for Black women, so being aware of and applying for these opportunities could have gone a long way in helping offset the financial burden. It's hard to get answers when you don't even know the right questions to ask.

Seeking out guidance from a financial aid counselor can help you make informed decisions about financing your education. Here are some of the major options you can discuss:

- Financial Aid
- Scholarships
- Work-Study Programs
- Student Loans

I put these options in order of my preference (free money over loans any day!), but let's go through the details of each one so you can make an informed decision about what's right for you.

## Financial Aid

Always start with free money first before taking out loans! The very first thing I recommend you do is fill out the Free Application for Federal Student Aid (FAFSA), which determines your eligibility for federal, state, and school-specific financial aid. While this is a federal application, many states, schools, and even some private lenders use it to determine whether you qualify for their aid programs. You need to fill out the FAFSA every year, but it's totally worth it since it gives you access to the greatest variety of funds to pay for college.

The FAFSA is need-based, which means it takes into consideration how much money you make (or your parents if you're a dependent) and how much your educational expenses are projected to be. The FAFSA requires you (or your parents) to submit financial information to determine what's reasonable for you (or your family) to pay toward your college expenses, and how much financial aid you need to make up the difference. You can apply for the FAFSA online, and most schools have financial aid counselors who can help you if you get stuck.

Federal Pell Grants are awarded to undergraduate students with the greatest economic needs. They don't need to be repaid, which is why I strongly encourage you to fill out the FAFSA and see if you're eligible for these funds. The maximum Pell Grant award can change from year to year, but it totaled $7,395 for the 2023–24 award year.[5] The exact amount you will receive up to the yearly maximum depends on several factors:

- Your expected family contribution
- The cost of attendance at your chosen school or program
- Your full-time or part-time student status
- Your plans for attending a full academic year or less

---

5    https://studentaid.gov/announcements-events/pell-max-award.

State financial aid helps residents further reduce their educational expenses by offering grants or scholarships. Often, these funds are distributed on a "first-come, first-served" basis, so getting your application in early is key.[6] You can find out more about your state's financial aid program, and whether you need to fill out an application in addition to the FAFSA, by contacting your state grant agency.[7]

Your school of choice will likely offer financial aid as well, which you can find on your college's financial aid website or by talking to a financial aid counselor at the institution. You might even be eligible for extra funds depending on your specific area of study, or the program you're interested in attending.[8]

## Scholarships

Scholarships are gifts that don't have to be repaid, just like financial aid. Some scholarships are based on economic need. Others are merit-based, meaning they're awarded to students who've excelled academically or have certain talents, skills, interests, or traits. You might be eligible for an athletic scholarship if you're a student-athlete, a STEM or arts grant, or funds based on your GPA or high SAT and ACT scores.[9]

Many scholarships are geared toward specific groups, such as nontraditional students, military families, women, or Black and indigenous people. It's a bit tricky to find applicable scholarships because there is no true one-stop shop that aggregates all opportunities, since schools, employers, nonprofits, religious groups, and professional organizations can all offer scholarships and grants. However, Scholly is one of the most comprehensive aggregator databases for

---

6   https://studentaid.gov/help-center/answers/article/state-aid.

7   https://www2.ed.gov/about/contacts/state/index.html.

8   https://financialaidtoolkit.ed.gov/tk/learn/types.jsp.

9   https://studentaid.gov/understand-aid/types/scholarships.

finding scholarships, discounts, and deals for college students.[10] Aside from the legitimate websites and organizations trying to help college students, there are also quite a few scams preying on prospective students.

To be safe, stick with the following for finding legitimate scholarship information:

- Your college's financial aid office (or your academic adviser if you're still in high school)
- Your state grant agency that also provides state-specific financial aid
- The US Department of Labor's free scholarship search tool[11]
- Professional organizations and associations related to your field of study
- Your employer, religious or community organizations, civic groups, or local foundations

## Work-Study Programs

Federal Work-Study offers part-time jobs for graduate and undergraduate students with economic need, usually in fields related to the student's educational focus. This is neither a gift like financial aid and scholarships nor a student loan, but simply another way to help you access funds for your educational expenses.[12]

Since you may already have a job (or multiple), why would you consider a work-study job over a regular part-time job? Regular jobs are likely to pay you more, but there are other benefits to taking on a work-study job instead:

- They're often related to your program and provide practical education

---

10   https://www2.myscholly.com/.

11   https://www.careeronestop.org/toolkit/training/find-scholarships.aspx.

12   https://studentaid.gov/understand-aid/types/work-study.

- They're frequently located on campus, reducing transportation problems
- They're generally more flexible when it comes to scheduling around your classes
- They don't affect your financial aid eligibility, while regular part-time job income does

## Student Loans

Student loans are funds you can borrow to cover the costs associated with higher education, including tuition, room and board, books, and supplies. They have to be paid back with interest. The government or private lenders that service the loans set the specific loan terms, interest rates, and repayment requirements.

The US Department of Education's federal student loan program provides different types of direct loans for graduate and undergraduate students, mostly based on financial need.[13] As an undergraduate student, you can borrow up to $12,500 per year at a fixed interest rate.

You can also choose from a variety of private student loan lenders, Sallie Mae being the largest one you may have heard of. You may need to go the private route if you can't cover your educational expenses with federal financial aid, scholarships, and loans, but make sure you read the fine print, as private loans are often less favorable to borrowers.

Benefits of federal student loans over private lender loans include:[14]

- You don't have to start repaying the loan until after you leave college
- You don't need to get a credit check to qualify
- The government subsidizes these loans by paying some of the interest

---

13   https://studentaid.gov/understand-aid/types/loans.

14   https://studentaid.gov/understand-aid/types/loans/federal-vs-private.

- You have more financial hardship options (such as loan forgiveness, deferment, and forbearance)[15]

Before you sign any loan documents, you need to know what type of loan you're getting (federal or private, subsidized or unsubsidized, etc.), your interest rate, grace and deferment periods, repayment plans and options, and impact on your credit. In any case, I highly recommend you borrow only what you absolutely need. Because student loans accrue interest over time, you'll increase the overall amount you owe significantly by starting out with a higher loan amount.

This is difficult, especially for low-income individuals and Black women, because we often have limited access to quality K–12 education, making our college applications less competitive, resulting in less financial aid and heavier reliance on student loans.

Even though these options are certainly more varied than I was aware of when I began my higher-education journey, financing a college degree still creates a lot of anxiety for most people.

## Managing Student Loans While Trying to Build Wealth (. . . And Sometimes Just Get By)

After graduation, many borrowers face financial difficulties when the high-paying jobs don't materialize. They end up stuck with large monthly payments while unemployed or barely scraping by, dealing with emergency expenses, or struggling with significant lifestyle changes such as divorce or becoming parents. We just don't have control over so many of the potential events or hardships that can severely impact our ability to repay student loans. I experienced several periods in my life when I couldn't make my student loan payments, which caused me a lot of anxiety.

---

15  Forgiveness: all or part of your student loans are discharged or canceled. Deferment: payments are postponed but in most cases continue to accrue interest. Forbearance: payments are suspended or reduced but in all cases continue to accrue interest.

Since then, I've learned that although it's scary to have student loan debt hanging over me, I'm not powerless. It's difficult but possible to manage student loan debt while building wealth. You might be tempted to ignore the payment reminders and lender communications if you're strapped for cash. However, dealing with the discomfort of facing the issue head-on today will result in peace of mind tomorrow.

## What to Do If You Can't Make Your Regular Payment

Student loan debt became the bogeyman that haunted my finances. It felt overwhelming and suffocating to even think about. Fear was the driving force behind my actions when paying off my debt. I didn't have a strategy, and I was unaware of the options available to manage the burden of student loans.

Any anger we may feel over the state of education in America is legitimate, yet we still must deal with this debt today so we can provide for our families. Once I started to educate myself on the facts of student loan debt, I realized that this bogeyman wasn't as invincible as I thought.

Here are the major options to consider when navigating student loan repayment:

1 Public Service Loan Forgiveness
2 Consolidation
3 Refinancing
4 Income-Based Repayment Plans

Let's walk through these options so you can get an idea of the strategy that's right for you. I could've advocated for myself better if I had known more. Looking back, I now understand how important it is to be proactive and communicate your situation with your loan servicer. I strongly encourage you to reach out. Your loan servicer can provide guidance and information about repayment plans, forgiveness programs, and any other assistance to navigate student loan debt and help you make more informed decisions.

If you're unsure who your loan servicer is and how to contact them, visit your account dashboard on studentaid.gov and scroll down to the "My Loan Servicers" section.[16] Or call the Federal Student Aid Information Center (FSAIC) at 1-800-433-3243. You can also ask the financial aid office at your college. In any case, never pay a company for help with negotiating your federal student loans. The loan servicers are required to help you for free.

## Public Service Loan Forgiveness

Public Service Loan Forgiveness (PSLF) could be an option for you if you meet certain criteria, such as working for a government or non-profit employer.[17] However, this program isn't the same as general student loan forgiveness, which was promised but not delivered by the Biden administration. PSLF has much more stringent eligibility guidelines, but it's worth it to check if you qualify:

- You must be employed full-time by a US federal, state, local, or tribal government or a registered 501(c)(3) nonprofit. Military service is also included.
- Your student loans must be a Direct Loan (or be eligible for consolidation into a Direct Loan—more on that below).
- You must be on an income-based repayment plan (reduced monthly payments based on how much you make) or a ten-year standard repayment plan (fixed monthly payments that aren't adjusted based on your income).
- You must have made a total of 120 qualifying monthly payments. Yes, that means having paid for ten years already, which is a very long time. The payments don't have to be consecutive, though, and the COVID-19 payment pause counts toward PSLF.

---

16    https://studentaid.gov/manage-loans/repayment/servicers.

17    https://studentaid.gov/manage-loans/forgiveness-cancellation/public-service.

## Consolidation

Consolidating student loans involves combining multiple federal education loans into a single Direct Consolidation Loan, usually with a fixed interest rate.[18] This is one of the types of loans you must hold to meet the requirements for PSLF.

Consolidation could have simplified the repayment process for me by merging different monthly payments into one, making it easier to keep track of and manage my student loan debt. Another benefit to consolidation is that it often allows for extending the repayment term, which lowers the monthly payment, providing some relief in dire financial situations.

One of the main disadvantages is that it will take you longer to pay off your loan, resulting in more payments and a higher interest cost over the term of the loan.

## Refinancing

This is the only strategy that's not offered through government services. You can refinance student loans only with a private lender. Refinancing is similar to consolidation but with one significant difference. Both consolidation and refinancing can combine multiple loans into one lower monthly payment by extending the repayment term. The big difference is that refinancing involves obtaining a new loan with better terms, such as a lower interest rate if you've improved your credit score since taking out the original loans. This could save you thousands of dollars in interest over the life of the loan.[19] However, one of the main disadvantages of refinancing is that you're no longer eligible for income-driven repayment plans (we'll discuss those next), or any other government-sponsored loan

---

18    https://studentaid.gov/manage-loans/consolidation.

19    https://www.bankrate.com/loans/student-loans/student-loans-refinance-federal-student-loans/#pros-cons.

forgiveness, deferment, or forbearance (pausing loan payments due to hardship).

Refinancing could have helped me take control of my student loan debt by reducing the overall cost and making it more manageable in the long run. Unfortunately, I had no clue about the terms of my student loans or even what my interest rates were. Financial sites such as NerdWallet[20] or Bankrate[21] offer online tools that help you comparison shop for refinancing options based on factors such as your home state, credit score, and loan amount. Then these sites help you compare interest rates, monthly payment amounts, fees, and repayment terms.

## Income-Based Repayment Plans

Exploring income-based repayment plans was a game changer for me, and my only regret is not knowing about this sooner. There are multiple plans under this umbrella, including:

- Saving on a Valuable Education (SAVE) Plan— formerly the REPAYE Plan
- Pay As You Earn (PAYE) Repayment Plan
- Income-Based Repayment (IBR) Plan
- Income-Contingent Repayment (ICR) Plan

All these plans calculate your monthly payment based on your income and family size, providing a more affordable repayment option for those facing financial hardship.[22] These plans may extend your repayment term up to twenty-five years, more than double the average ten years of a regular loan repayment term. Income-driven plans can help adjust your monthly payments to a manageable level, usually not more than 10 percent of your discretionary income. You can meet your

---

20  https://nerdwallet.com/refinancing-student-loans.

21  https://www.bankrate.com/loans/student-loans/refinance-rates/.

22  https://studentaid.gov/manage-loans/repayment/plans/income-driven.

basic living expenses while still making progress on your student loan debt. This was the option that I decided to go with. It made the most sense for my circumstances and allowed me to start chipping away at my student loans with the money I had available.

## Communication Is Key

Years ago, I was so overwhelmed with the burden of my student loans that I found myself either not taking action at all and ignoring the bills or making payments with money I didn't have, all because I had heard horror stories about the long-term consequences of student loan debt.

Defaulting on your student loans can lead to severe penalties, including damaging your credit score, wage garnishment, and potential legal action. I didn't know this, because I was too scared to ask, but ignoring my student loans and running from the bogeyman wasn't going to help me—it only amplified the problem.

I finally reached out to my loan servicer to explore my options. I was honest. I laid out the reality of my finances, including that I was broke and needed a low-cost, low-effort option to get rid of my student loans. I expressed my fear of the consequences for defaulting on my loan, including jail time.

I now know that jail time isn't a punishment for unpaid student loan debt but a persistent myth that caused me unnecessary stress and fear. This type of misinformation can spread and have an impact on our emotional and mental well-being. By being transparent, I opened the door for a constructive and informative conversation.

The loan servicer was empathetic and explained to me that serious consequences such as wage garnishment are also rare and happen only in extreme cases when an account has been delinquent for many months. They explained that student loans were not a criminal offense, and their goal was to assist borrowers like me with finding solutions rather than punishing or imprisoning me. Loan servicers primarily want to collect money, and a little is better than nothing, so it's in their best business interest to work with borrowers as much as possible.

## Figuring Out the Best Strategy to Pay Off Your Student Loans

When you're well-informed, seek guidance, and explore all available options to manage your student loan debt, you're more likely to make choices that align with your financial goals and provide the best path toward a debt-free future. Standard repayment plan terms are usually ten years, so if you can swing the fixed monthly payment, you'll be able to pay off your debt in a decade. However, the pressure to prioritize student loan repayment above all else can lead to unnecessary and damaging sacrifices to your financial well-being. You can't, and don't have to, let that happen. Step back and consider your bigger financial picture. While it's important not to ignore student loan debt completely, you can approach repayment with a strategic mindset so you can balance your daily expenses and maintain financial stability. For most of us, our income fluctuates depending on life events, such as getting a new job, having a kid, getting married, or falling ill. Income-based repayment plans adjust your monthly payment amounts based on your changing income by extending your repayment period to twenty or more years, allowing you to make progress while giving you room to breathe. But this also means that you will take much longer to eliminate your debt and end up paying more in interest.

After considering my options, the income-based repayment plan worked best for me. I paid what I could comfortably afford each month while still covering my essential expenses. It's crucial to set realistic payment amounts that won't strain your budget to the point where you're sacrificing necessities or falling into further debt. This means considering the need for emergency savings, retirement contributions, and other long-term financial plans.

When I took out my loans, I didn't think beyond college to consider the long-term impact of student loan debt on my financial future. I didn't think about how repaying the loans could affect my other financial goals.

## Balancing Wealth Building with Student Loan Repayment

Student loan debt can significantly impact other financial goals, such as buying a home, purchasing a car, saving for retirement, or starting a family. Delaying these goals temporarily while managing the debt can be a viable strategy, especially because most lenders for mortgages or car loans take into consideration your existing debt, credit score, and income. They pay special attention to what's called your debt-to-income ratio. This means that the dollar amount you owe on your student loans is less important than how much your monthly debt payments are in comparison to your income. The same dollar amount debt payment isn't going to be a problem for someone with a higher income, but it could be the deciding factor in whether a low-income person qualifies for a home mortgage.

If you don't want to delay your goals, it's crucial to consider every possible avenue to reduce your overall student loan debt or monthly payments so you have a higher portion of your income available for saving, investing, wealth building, and achieving your other big-picture goals. Student loans are also the hardest to discharge during bankruptcy, requiring you to prove undue hardship, which is difficult to do and therefore extremely rare to be approved. This means that you'll have to deal with your student loans sooner or later, because they're almost impossible to get rid of. In other words, any progress you make on reducing your student loan debt is an important step toward financial freedom and building wealth.

Struggling with student loans is not just about the numbers on the loan statements, but the emotional toll it takes on you. The burden of student loan debt, paired with the lack of high-paying jobs available, can feel like a dark cloud hovering over you at all times. Even if you're familiar with the available resources, it's not always about the money as much as the feeling of dread or hopelessness.

We often hear stories of people paying off enormous amounts of debt in short periods of time, so it's easy to get trapped in the comparison game. You may compare yourself to people who have either paid off their student loans much quicker than you or have been able to translate their degree into dollars. There have been plenty of times when I've regretted having gone to school in the first place, even though I value the experiences and education I received.

When you have student loan debt, it's easy to feel guilty for not being able to financially contribute to your family in the ways you would like, such as buying a car, purchasing a home, or even having more children. The guilt around having to take money out of my household budget to pay for an education I never completed used to eat away at me. I've found comfort in accepting that education, whether it results in a degree or not, is a worthy investment, though sometimes risky. I no longer let guilt and regret overshadow the courage it took for me to continue my education and now to manage the resulting debt.

In addition to strategically managing my own student loan debt, I'm taking steps to ensure my two sons won't have to follow in my footsteps. I learned about 529 college savings plans, which allow me to invest small amounts of money each month into an investment account that accrues compound interest without incurring taxes on those earnings. Even though I didn't have much money to spare, the 529 plans earn more interest than if I just put that money into high-yield savings accounts for my boys, which yield 4.5–5.3% interest.[23] Because 529 plans invest your contributions into stocks and bonds, you won't know exactly how much your return on investment will be, but

---

23   https://www.forbes.com/advisor/banking/savings/best-high-yield-savings-accounts/.

the annual stock market return has been just over 10 percent since its inception almost seven decades ago. More importantly, if I choose to take the money out of the 529 for a qualified educational expense, the withdrawals will also be tax-free, instead of paying the average 15 percent income tax[24] on the money I saved for my boys. The power of compounding interest and tax-free growth is making a difference for my sons' future even if I can spare only $20 a month.

Worrying about my student loans used to affect my mood, sleep, and overall well-being. The bogeyman was always waiting in the dark closet or under the bed, ready to attack, keeping me up at night. Facing that bogeyman made all the difference.

I wasn't powerless after all, and neither are you.

## Checklist—What to Ask About Obtaining Financing and Managing Loan Repayment

### 1. FINANCIAL AID

- What types of financial aid are available to me (grants, scholarships, loans, work-study), and how do I apply?
- What are the specific academic or extracurricular requirements?
- How is financial need assessed for each option?
- Can I appeal a financial aid decision if my situation changes?

### 2. LOANS

- What types of student loans are available to me (federal, private, etc.)?
- How do I compare interest rates, fees, and payment terms to find the best option for me?
- Are there any academic performance requirements to maintain the loan?

---

24  https://taxfoundation.org/data/all/federal/latest-federal-income-tax-data-2024
/#:~:text=The%20average%20income%20tax%20rate,the%20bottom%20half%20of%20
taxpayers.

## 3. APPLICATION PROCESS

- What documents and information do I need to gather to apply for financial aid and student loans?
- What are the application deadlines, and how long does the process typically take?

## 4. REPAYMENT PLANS

- What repayment plans are available, including income-driven options?
- Can I switch repayment plans, and if so, how often?
- What options are available if I face financial hardship (deferment, forbearance, etc.)?
- When does repayment officially begin?
- Are there any penalties for early repayment of the loan?

## 5. MANAGING MULTIPLE LOANS

- If I have multiple loans, can I consolidate them?
- How does consolidation affect interest rates and repayment terms?
- What are the pros and cons of loan consolidation?
- What are the benefits and drawbacks of refinancing my student loans?
- How do I compare different refinancing options and lenders to choose the best option for me?

## 6. LOAN FORGIVENESS AND DISCHARGE

- Are there any loan forgiveness programs I might qualify for, and what are their requirements?
- Under what circumstances, if any, can my loans be discharged?

# CHAPTER 5

# Kids Change Your Life, and Your Wallet (Parenting)

My cousin's face tensed up when she confided in me how worried she was about taking a pregnancy test. She was so scared to see the outcome that she couldn't bring herself to take the test alone. In the spur of the moment, I decided the best way to support my cousin would be to take a test with her. I'm not sure why I thought this would help. We were both naive nineteen-year-old girls, and it just felt like the right thing to do. Little did I know that my gesture of support would lead to me standing in my cousin's bathroom only minutes later, staring down at two pink lines on a positive pregnancy test. Except it wasn't my cousin's test. It was mine.

I was shocked and disappointed. The timing couldn't have been worse. I'd just dropped out of college for the first time, and my mom had pulled a few strings to get me a full-time job with benefits at the insurance company where she worked. I was just starting to get my financial footing as a young adult, and now I was on my way to becoming someone's mom. It was so overwhelming. I already understood some of the difficulties of being a very young parent, since my parents had me when they were teens. I also knew, that day in my cousin's bathroom, that I was still a very long way from being financially secure enough to support a child.

Those two pink lines were my starting point to understanding just how much kids change our lives, and our perspectives around money. Now I joke that had I not become pregnant at nineteen, I'd still be living for the weekend. That was my reality at the time. I was bored with my daily life and used to spending money however I wanted and worrying about the resulting problems later. Getting pregnant was the wake-up call I needed to stop living paycheck to paycheck and invest effort into planning for a future that now included a baby.

As I write this, that baby I first found out about as a scared teen is now a sophomore in high school with his own bank account, budget, and financial priorities. His little brother is in middle school and also runs his own budget, helps strategize our grocery spending, and has an emergency fund. I am so proud of us and the village that has helped us become financially secure. When conventional money advice didn't apply to me and my family situation, I discovered the strategies I share in this chapter that *did* work to keep us on firm financial ground.

My most profound realization as a young, single mom who forged my own path to financial security is that *everyone* has the power to create a financially sound future for their family. This isn't a privilege that's reserved for the rich. Mainstream conversations about money can trick us into believing that setting our kids up for financial success requires bloated trust funds or huge wealth transfers, but I'm here to tell you—and show you—that's just not true. Some of the most effective ways we can set our kids up for success don't even require an exchange of money. They involve showing up for our family through daily actions, education, and support that empower them to become financially independent. Nobody set that example for me more than my mom. And it started the moment she found out that my baby boy was on his way.

## Embrace Your Village

Not everyone is blessed with a big family or community who can support them. But sometimes even a village of one can make all the difference to someone's financial future. Often we strive to feel empowered and confident in our ability to manage our finances on our own. However, there are times when we have no choice but to handle everything on our own, which can be challenging. Accepting help doesn't diminish our strength, it enhances our ability to succeed. When we face financial difficulties, the pressure to solve everything on our own can lead to stress, burnout, and resentment. Embracing your village is a strategic way to overcome obstacles, not a sign of weakness. As parents, one of the best ways we can help our children get ahead financially is by showing up for them at their most vulnerable. As kids, one of the best things we can do for ourselves and our own children is to accept help even when we'd prefer to show the world that we can handle challenges on our own. My mom was my village of one when I found out I was going to be a mother, and she showed up for my son and me in a way that improved our lives immeasurably.

When I first told my mom that I was pregnant, she was reassuring but cautious. She fully supported my decision to go through with my pregnancy but expressed her desire for me to have a better life than she did as a teen mom. She would do everything in her power to help set me up for success but made it clear there would be certain obstacles and challenges I might not be able to avoid even with the most supportive family. She knew how hard it was to be a young, single, Black mother.

What she did next gave me and my son the financial head start that helped us survive the hard early years, and we're still benefiting from her actions now, over a decade later. She'd just set me up with a great job at the insurance company where she worked when I found out I was pregnant. My mom made sure I excelled personally and professionally in that predominantly white environment as a young, Black, pregnant woman. I was the youngest employee in the entire company and relied on my mom to teach me how to navigate corporate America. She had my back in every way.

I spent the next nine months working through my pregnancy, simultaneously learning to navigate the workforce and health-care system with all the complexities of race, gender, and expecting a child. Those identities shaped my experience, and I was grateful to have my mom by my side to guide me. Studies show that Black women are more likely to receive inadequate prenatal care, face higher rates of preterm labor and complications during delivery, and are nearly three times more likely than white women to die during childbirth.[1] These statistics weighed heavily on me, but they weren't the only thing on my mind. I also experienced the social stigma against pregnant teenagers firsthand and faced my coworkers' stereotypes and judgments. From the questions people asked me, like "Are you married?" to side glances and hushed conversation when I walked into the room, I often felt embarrassed, not only for myself, but also for my mom. I'm sure it had been difficult for her, especially since we worked together, but she always stood up for me.

Despite society's pressure to punish young mothers into learning from their "mistakes" on their own by offering no guidance and support, my mom did the complete opposite. She made a selfless decision that helped lay the foundation for my children and me, shaping our lives in immeasurable ways for years to come.

My mom's next piece of advice surprised me: toward the end of my pregnancy, she suggested I quit my job and move back home so I could

---

1    https://www.ncbi.nlm.nih.gov/pmc/articles/PMC9914526/#:~:text=Black%20women%20
have%20a%20maternal,racial%20disparities%20persist%20%5B54%5D.

focus on being a mother while she took care of our expenses. Mom had helped me get that first apartment as a cosigner when I was only eighteen and had no credit history to apply for a rental on my own. It was a beyond generous offer to move back in with her, but I felt conflicted about giving up my own place, quitting my job, and not contributing financially while my mom shouldered the burden for all of us. I'd also done well in my job and was worried about my prospects if I quit. But my mom saw the bigger picture. She was confident I could reenter the corporate world when I was ready to go back, because she saw me build the skills and relationships required to thrive in that environment. But for the time being, I needed to focus on motherhood. Eventually, I took her advice, quit my job, and moved back in with her.

Mom took care of me and my newborn son. She taught me everything about emotionally, mentally, physically, and financially caring for a child. My bills decreased drastically, because I no longer had rent, utility, or grocery expenses. On top of that, my mom paid for my personal expenses like hygiene products and a prepaid cell phone plan. Most importantly, she covered everything my son needed. I didn't have to worry about buying baby supplies, including diapers and formula, two incredibly expensive items. Parenthood can be so tough, and I'm immensely grateful that my mom made that transition so much gentler. Still, having a little one depending on me brought a whole new level of seriousness to my efforts to become financially stable. It was no longer about my own desires or immediate gratification.

I didn't want to embody the preconceptions of financial irresponsibility and limited opportunities that usually accompany teen pregnancy. I didn't want my children to face the same struggles that my mom faced with me. I wanted them to have a better start in life and a stronger financial foundation to set them up for success. My mom and I were determined to break the cycle and make sure my children and her grandchildren would be raised on a foundation of financial security and safety.

Because of my mom's generosity, I was able to use those months we lived with her to better my overall financial situation. I took a night job at McDonald's and worked almost forty hours a week. Going from a desk job to flipping burgers may seem like a drastic change to some, but it was the best decision I could have made for that season of my life. I can't stress enough how supportive and nonjudgmental my new working environment was and how welcome I felt there. On top of that, McDonald's gave me flexible hours to earn and save money while I learned to be a mom. Together with my mom covering our expenses, this job allowed me to get my life back on track. I was in a much more stable position financially when I went out on my own again—this time as a new mom.

I understand I was incredibly blessed to have my mom's support as a new parent. Many people in my same situation would not have had that opportunity. But even if your family dynamic looks nothing like mine did, we can all relate to needing a little help from our village when we're feeling lost. I eventually learned to navigate the tension between my desire to grow financially independent and to lean on my village for support. I'm finally in a position where I get to be a part of the supportive village for extended family and friends. I'm now in my mid-thirties, the same age as my mother when she took care of me and my newborn son. At the time, she was still figuring out her career and didn't have a big financial cushion. She didn't hold an executive position at her company either. Yet she gave to the village what she could. She pulled all the levers and gave me push after push toward financial stability, whether it was by buying my deodorant and shampoo or letting us live rent-free in her house.

I keep repeating how even the smallest act of kindness can be enough to change your or someone else's financial experience or even life trajectory, because I've seen it work in my life and my family's lives. From small to big actions, my mom shared her resources without sitting on a giant trust fund, being established in her own career, or having disposable income. Look for those moments to help and to accept help. They can make all the difference.

## Creating a Living Legacy

I moved out when my son was nine months old. I settled into a new, larger apartment with my paid-off car and a much better position at my previous company, where I was rehired after my extended maternity leave. That position ended up being my foot in the door of financial literacy, which eventually led to me starting The Broke Black Girl. None of this would have happened if it wasn't for my mom's love and generosity. She's truly my best example of creating what I call a living legacy. This is the act of helping our younger family members create financial stability through everyday gestures of support. Creating a living legacy is not about huge wealth transfers, because, let's face it, that's not the norm for most people. Just like my mom, you can do this without signing a huge check or leaving your kid with a trust fund. It's much simpler and more accessible than that. Building a living legacy can be any action that helps alleviate the financial barriers you or your family face. Sometimes, they'll be monumental actions like my mom's offer for me to move back home, but more often they'll be small, daily actions that accumulate over time.

My mom created a living legacy by learning to be financially secure herself and then passing on that knowledge and support to me. Now I'm developing financial security and teaching my own kids to do the same, continuing on down the generations of our family, deepening my mom's original act of love. My mom stood in the gap for me again and again when I needed her. That's not spoiling a child but creating a safety net and proper guidance without enabling permanent dependence. I would do the same for my kids, and I try to be there for them and young family members in smaller ways right now. I believe this approach strikes a balance between supporting our kids and encouraging self-sufficiency so we can help them avoid unnecessary struggles and become financially responsible in the long term.

However, you need to ensure that your support of others doesn't come at the expense of developing your own financial stability.

## Small, Daily Actions Lead to Big Future Impacts

This is the same approach I take to teaching my kids or giving advice to my online readers. When it comes to talking about generational wealth, we gotta keep it real and include everyone, no matter their income bracket. I don't even like the term "generational wealth" in the way that it's often used today because it comes off as intimidating and exclusionary, which is why I like to talk about building a living legacy. Instead of one grand gesture that wasn't within my reach, I made small, daily choices that added up to building financial security for myself while teaching my kids, family members, and other young Black women online.

It can seem overwhelming when you realize, just like I did, that I wouldn't be able to apply conventional money advice like saving the recommended 20 percent of my income for an emergency fund. However, putting in the 2 percent instead eventually got me there too. This goes for basics like budget planning, savings, retirement, and emergency funds, but also for onetime expenses, experiences, and special occasions.

Once you realize your small actions will snowball into significant returns, it gets fun. When my older son started his freshman year of high school, I started planning for his senior year. Senior trips, prom, graduation party, and gifts, senior pictures and announcements—it can all get overwhelmingly expensive. Spending money on extras like vacations or your child's senior-year events and celebrations shouldn't mean neglecting other financial responsibilities. By starting to save early for senior-year expenses, you can meet all your financial obligations while still providing your child with a memorable and enjoyable experience. A low-cost, low-effort, low-stress strategy is automatically putting $25–$35 a week into a high-yield savings account when your child starts high school and then letting compound interest do its thing until senior year. Depending on your savings account interest, you could accumulate $3,750–$5,250 by the time you need the money. Of course, you can adjust the weekly amount down or up depending on your situation. Over time, even a little will go a long way.

Imagine how much more fun you'll have when the money you set aside allows you to focus on celebrating your child's achievement rather than stressing about paying for everything. I model this approach while teaching my sons through introducing developmentally appropriate small actions they can practice.

## Age-Appropriate Money Concepts and Activities

One of the greatest gifts you can give your children is to prepare them to be financially empowered adults. Teaching children to be financially responsible early on will help them overcome preventable financial challenges like overspending, not creating a practical spending plan, getting into debt, or being unable to resist impulsive expenses and spending triggers. Here are some of the most actionable, tangible, and manageable money concepts we can teach our kids. A little each day, in age-appropriate ways, will instill money wisdom in them that will last a lifetime.

| Ages 5–7 | Ages 8–12 |
|---|---|
| Basic math: counting, adding, and subtracting coins | Opening a bank account with parental help |
| Using three jars for "Save," "Spend," and "Share" | Setting a savings goal for a desired item |
| Singing songs about saving money | Earning an allowance for ongoing chores |
| Giving small allowances for simple chores | Shopping with a budget and list |
| Answering money questions age-appropriately | Micro-philanthropy (small charitable giving or volunteering in your community) |

| Ages 13–15 | Ages 16–18 |
|---|---|
| Understanding how borrowing, interest, and loans work | Learning about different college funding options |
| Creating a personal budget with income vs. expenses | Helping them understand how investing works |
| Earning money through casual jobs | Understanding the real cost of a home (mortgage, insurance, interest, upkeep, emergencies) |
| Understanding the true cost of owning a car (vehicle, insurance, maintenance, registration, etc.) | Discussing financial independence |
| Understanding the difference between wants and needs | Learning about the overall expenses of a household and how to manage them |
| Developing critical thinking skills to evaluate advertising messages and the constant consumption culture on social media | Understanding wages and salaries of their part-time jobs, including tax information |
| | Monetizing skills and talents |

In my family, age-appropriate money discussions go hand in hand with direct support and sharing of resources. My mom taught me how to utilize what she had to give me a hand up, so I emphasize this approach with my own kids.

Teaching kids about money is 10 percent knowledge and 90 percent imitation. Your kids will pick up your beliefs and attitudes about money. They soak up everything—the good, the bad, and the ugly. What you *say* about money, the words you use, your tone, body language, and facial expressions (even if you're "just joking") are as important as what you *do* with money. Growing up, I heard many adults around me swear off credit cards. I didn't know the first thing about credit cards and never had a bad experience, but I retained those beliefs well into adulthood. So much of how we experience, value, and manage money is based on our history, our families' beliefs, and what we've been taught. It took me years to undo that vague fear of credit cards that wasn't based on any facts or personal experience. This is only one of the many money stories I grew up with that I actively had to question to prevent passing them on to my own kids.

Aside from dismantling these cultural or family stories, I give my kids opportunities to practice the skills they've learned at home outside in the real world.

## Teach Your Kids Real-World Money Skills

There are many practical ways to teach your kids how to gradually take on more financial responsibility as they mature. I'm still recovering from the day my mom told me I needed to start paying my cell phone bill. That was the day I found out I was grown for real. Hasn't been the same since.

You can teach your kids at any age about financial concepts in developmentally appropriate ways that help them build a solid financial foundation and develop a healthy relationship with money. Since my older son turned thirteen, I've given him a different weekly challenge for life skills related to money management to get him out of his comfort zone and used to living independently. To take financial responsibility for a family or contribute to a community, we all must learn personal financial responsibility first. It's okay to start small and work your way up.

One week, my son's task was picking up clothes from the cleaners and using a credit card to pay for the services, sign the receipt, and politely interact with the clerk. I'm always there to guide him in these situations and make sure to remind him to use eye contact, speak up, put his phone down, and take his AirPods out so he can pay attention. He was so proud when he got back into the car, where I was waiting for him. The week after that, we went grocery shopping with a list and a budget.

It's crucial to prepare our teenagers for the real world through actual experiences because they will gain invaluable skills and knowledge that will help them communicate, problem-solve, interact with others, make good decisions, budget, manage their time, and take care of themselves. Most importantly, real-world experiences under the guidance of a loving adult will help kids and teenagers develop confidence in their abilities and trust in their own judgment.

My mom's hands-on approach with me had a lasting impact on how I parent by inspiring me to pass down the same principles to my children, especially when it comes to money management. Children repeat what they see their parents doing. They soak up everything. Of course, each child is an individual with a different personality, giving me an opportunity to adapt my approach. My older son, for example, spends his money more freely than my younger son, who's more likely to save his allowance. Neither one is better or worse. Sound money management includes both saving and spending funds, but recognizing their different patterns allows me to be more strategic about which money conversation to bring up next depending on their most immediate needs.

Often, that strategic conversation will need to go hand in hand with practical support, but that doesn't necessarily mean you'll have to pay for everything.

## How to Support Your Kids Financially Without Cash

My mom taught me how to leverage resources to help the next generation move ahead financially. Even when we don't have any actual money to give, there are so many ways you can make an impact through small and significant actions while teaching your kids and other young family members financial responsibility. Many of these won't cost you anything but your time:

- Help them gather important identity documents, like birth certificates and Social Security cards, so they have all their information in one place for applications (work, school, loans).
- Offer rides or babysitting so transportation and childcare and
  their related financial burdens don't create a barrier to education or employment.
- Find scholarships for them to apply for to pay for school,
  easing their student loan burden and giving them more opportunities to pursue higher education.
- Add them as authorized users on your credit cards (without
  actually giving them a physical card!) to help them build their
  credit history without messing up yours.
- Share resources (books, educational materials, subscriptions, or
  networks) to give them access they wouldn't have on their own.

I know not all families can operate in this way, because in addition to money, your other resources, like time and energy, may also
be depleted. However, even incorporating a few of these gestures, no
matter how small they seem on the surface, can have the potential to
break the cycle of financial barriers the kids, teens, and young adults in
your life face. I try to help however it makes most sense for me at the
time, depending on the specific needs and circumstances of my family
members.

The point is to use what we already have at our disposal, no matter
how small it may seem, to push our children or younger family members ahead little by little.

I'm now in a position where I can make room in my budget to
cover my cousin's grocery costs while he's away at college. It's a small
portion of his overall educational expenses, but that's what I can do,
and it's one less thing he has to worry about while he's focusing on
his future. I also cover my niece's gymnastics class to offer her opportunities for personal growth, physical activity, socialization, and

just plain fun! I want her to know that I value her interests and am willing to support her passions. These are just a few small examples of what you can do, but they can look completely different for your situation.

These aren't grand gestures, but they do have ripple effects outside the person directly benefiting from your support. My cousin is one of seven children, and his family is grappling with the recent death of one of his siblings. On the surface, this is about groceries for a college kid, but one level deeper, it's also about creating a living legacy by supporting my aunt, his mom, who now has one less thing to worry about while freeing up time and mental space to heal and grieve.

Supporting my niece's passion for gymnastics is a profound way I honor my own childhood dreams. I grew up loving tennis and wanted nothing more than to be Serena Williams. However, tennis and any other extracurricular activities weren't in my parents' budget. I know what it's like to have a burning desire to try something new but be unable to because of money constraints. I want my niece to have a different experience without my sister bearing that mom guilt or stretching herself too thin financially.

While these expressions of care should come without strings attached, it's just as important to teach our kids the value of all our and other people's unseen or unpaid labor that benefits them.

## Small Lessons, Every Day, Teach Our Kids to See the Big Picture

A surprising outcome of teaching our kids about financial responsibility in small ways is that, little by little, all those lessons add up and help them understand the bigger picture. Once again, the most impactful lessons don't require us to pay for anything. We just need to help our kids see how certain actions have a ripple effect on our finances—and very often, other people's as well.

An important way I've been able to help my sons see the bigger picture is by educating them on unseen, unpaid labor. This is especially important as they're growing up with a single mom. I deeply appreciate the sacrifices my mom made for me, but it wasn't until I became a parent myself that it really hit home how much invisible work she did. It doesn't help that we're steeped in a culture that doesn't fully recognize the unpaid labor of women, especially single mothers.

It's important to me to show my boys the emotional labor, planning, and endless support and encouragement that are all components of maintaining a thriving family dynamic and functioning household. Usually, that's a burden society places on women without much expectation for men to carry equal weight. I am working hard to raise boys who contribute to a more just and equal society and to instill a curiosity for questioning and challenging all types of societal norms, whether based on gender, race, or class. I want my boys to understand that their worth is not solely determined by traditional notions of masculinity but rather by their ability to be empathetic and actively involved in all aspects of life.

There is no limitation or restriction in our home on who takes on certain responsibilities or enjoys certain rights or opportunities. Having these conversations is essential in preparing my sons to become conscious and engaged partners in their future relationships. I teach them that equity in a household goes beyond the division of visible tasks and includes recognizing and sharing unseen responsibilities. I believe true liberation starts at home when we don't expect ourselves or our children to confine themselves to predefined roles. Instead, we create a sense of flexibility and adaptability in the face of evolving societal norms.

Here's just one example that made me realize why teaching the value of unpaid work is my number one money lesson for my sons. It was the day of an important football practice for my older son, and despite my multiple reminders, he forgot his shirt. Can you believe it? A teenager forgetting something?!

Now, here's where things got real. I had to rearrange my meetings, scramble to find a replacement shirt (costing me both time and money), and rush it to his school. By the time I made it back home, I had to run out to get his little brother, cook dinner, and prepare for the next day. It meant pushing my professional tasks late into the night, leaving me running on fumes and working until 2 a.m., getting only four hours of sleep, and getting back up at 6 a.m.

This is just one small, everyday example of the immense value of unpaid work and the ripple effect caused by a small oversight. Teens forget stuff, so this wasn't about guilt-tripping my child over an honest mistake or burdening him with caregiving duties that belong to me as his mom. However, it was an opportunity to talk about shared responsibility and help him recognize the unseen labor that supports our daily lives. Sometimes it's me, and sometimes it's someone else, but I want my sons to have a deep understanding that there's always someone shouldering the load, even when it's unseen and unpaid.

By instilling a sense of empathy, respect, and shared responsibility in my sons, I'm fostering a household and family where we appreciate each other's contributions. We understand that a simple oversight can disrupt someone else's day, particularly the caregiver's. This comes down to cultivating awareness and gratitude, encouraging everyone to play their part.

Teaching my kids the ripple effect of their actions is also helpful in a greater communal and societal context. They're becoming more aware of what type of work and workers our culture values or ignores. They're beginning to see who has access to economic opportunities and gets fairly compensated for their contributions and who doesn't. Empathy and respect for this unseen or unpaid labor is only the first step. Next is teaching our children how to advocate for the economic needs of others, which is taking their sense of shared household responsibility and applying it to our community and society as a whole.

They become acutely aware of their place in the world and how their actions can have an impact on the people around them. Understanding and respecting the needs of other family members helps them recognize the importance of economic equity and advocate for financial justice. Whether it's joining a volunteer organization, writing letters to their local representatives, donating to or fundraising for a cause close to their hearts, there are many age-appropriate ways for your kids to speak up and take action. They gain a deeper understanding of the complexities of economic systems and how they can use their voice to make a difference.

Never underestimate the transformational effect of getting your finances right and then passing that legacy down so that, one by one, our families, communities, and countries are changed too. Sometimes we won't feel motivated to change until a life experience or chance encounter shifts our perspective. When this happens, it can be life-altering. For me, most of those moments were parenting-related, but they don't have to be. They can be triggered by all kinds of life events or small interactions. A big aha moment that motivated me to keep our finances in order came out of a conversation with my younger son that had nothing to do with money, or even parenting. We were in our kitchen when he noticed that I'd forgotten to properly turn off an electric burner. I thanked him for reminding me and said I didn't want him to be sad if I hurt myself. His response hit me hard: he said he wouldn't only be sad because I hurt myself, but he would be disappointed because I knew better and didn't do better.

It was tough for me to hear from my child that I didn't live up to writer Maya Angelou's admonition: *When you know better, do better.* His words resonated so much that I wanted to apply them to everything I could. There is information readily available at our fingertips that can help us do our best—financially or otherwise. We have the power to know better so that we can do better. Let's do all we can, because our good choices influence many people in our lives.

# Get Your Child Ready for the Real World
## Checklist of Financial Concepts to Teach Your Kids Before They Turn Eighteen

You don't have to be an expert. Share what you know, show them what you do, have a conversation, or learn together by watching videos, attending classes, and reading books. The best gift you can give your child is the opportunity to learn—together.

### 1. MONEY MANAGEMENT

- Creating a monthly budget
- Tracking income & expenses
- Setting financial goals
- Planning for emergencies
- Saving money
- Paying bills on time and the consequences of late payments
- Understanding credit scores and how to build and improve credit
- Understanding how interest works

### 2. MONEY PSYCHOLOGY

- Learning to distinguish needs from wants
- Understanding how to use credit cards responsibly
- Understanding your own risk tolerance and aversion
- Understanding the concepts of risk and reward, instant and delayed gratification
- Understanding the financial implications of real life vs. social media lifestyles
- Recognizing persuasive tactics in ads

### 3. FINANCIAL ETHICS

- Understanding consumer rights
- Understanding credit rights

- Avoiding predatory lending
- Avoiding scams and fraud, including identity theft and protecting sensitive information
- Reading and understanding contracts
- Paying attention to the fine print instead of "accepting" terms and conditions
- Asking questions before signing anything
- Understanding the implication of their legal signature once they're eighteen
- Advocating for financial justice and an equitable society (donating, volunteering)

# CHAPTER 6

# More Money, Same Problems (Lifestyle Inflation)

**Y**ou're acting like a person that ain't never had nothing!"
I'd heard this expression so many times growing up that it took me a while to realize when I became a walking example. While that phrase is usually a critique of someone's bad financial management by overspending on items they can't afford, I now see another aspect too. I had lived paycheck to paycheck for years, then spent nine months back home with my mom, saving diligently for a fresh start while preparing to become a mom. When my income finally surpassed my expenses, I encountered a new challenge. My salary had increased significantly after my previous employer rehired me in a better position, as a loan accountant rather than my original role of customer service representative, which led to an immediate change in my lifestyle.

I understand why and how people fall into the trap of lifestyle inflation so easily because I experienced it myself. If you've lived in long-term deprivation and poverty, maybe for generations, it only makes sense to try to compensate for past struggles. Suddenly, I was tempted to indulge in more of everything—clothes, shoes, jewelry, entertainment, and travel experiences. Most of all, I wanted to provide my son with everything I felt he deserved that I didn't have growing up. Did my one-year-old really need a pair of diamond earrings, the latest sneakers, and brand-name clothes? No, but this wasn't just a financial management issue; it was a complicated psychological and social dynamic. If you can't meet your own or your kids' needs for such a long time and then suddenly get access to financial resources, it makes sense that you're going to eat like you've been starving. This may manifest in buying luxury items, costly experiences, or status symbols of success.

I knew it wasn't the smartest financial decision, but my heart frequently overrode rational thoughts. Sometimes lifestyle inflation looks like a tangible sign of breaking the poverty cycle, even when it can trap us further down the road. We're all naturally inclined to seek instant gratification and immediate rewards over future benefits. This tug-of-war caused me increased impulse spending and lifestyle inflation.

## What Is Lifestyle Inflation?

Lifestyle inflation is the tendency to increase spending as your income goes up. This can lead to a cycle of never-ending consumption, where the more you earn, the more you spend, shifting your focus from building wealth to accumulating material possessions and luxury experiences. We all face societal pressure to signal our status by showing off material possessions. Our culture has a built-in lifestyle inflation trap. Combining those outside influences with a lack of understanding of budgeting, saving, and investing makes it even more likely that we'll overspend without planning for the future.

I personally experienced this when I began earning more in my career. At that time, I felt the need to upgrade everything around me. I was buying the latest technology, switching to premium brands, and dining at upscale restaurants more frequently. My closet was over-flowing with outfits I didn't need, I upgraded my apartment decor to match my "successful" lifestyle, and I found myself splurging on week-end getaways to treat myself after a stressful week. Although I ap-peared to have my financial act together—diligently saving, investing, building emergency funds, and paying off debt—the reality was that my spending was outpacing my income. These purchases were meant to reward myself for my hard work, but they soon became a false sense of financial security. Without realizing it, I was caught up in consum-erism, focusing more on the image of financial success rather than the reality of securing my financial future.

Growing up, it seemed that "inflating your lifestyle" was the ex-pectation when you finally started to make more money. I thought I was supposed to eventually get a bigger house and nicer car and buy that Gucci purse that makes me feel like I've "made it." The idea that increased income should automatically translate into a more extravagant lifestyle is deeply ingrained in many cultures, and breaking free from this mindset requires a conscious effort, whether you're single, partnered, or a parent. Before I knew it, "Do you have McDonald's money?" would turn into "Do you have crab legs money?" with my boys.

High-end items tend to feel like justified rewards for hard work and success. However, lifestyle inflation causes long-term impacts on financial stability and the ability to achieve important life goals, such as saving for retirement, investing, or buying a home. Keeping your personal values in mind can also help you ensure your spend-ing is aligned with your long-term goals, rather than spur-of-the-moment desires.

When discussing inflation, we often focus on rising prices and the cost of living, including how much more we spend on housing, gas, groceries, and basic consumer goods. We can't control this type of economic inflation, but we can control lifestyle inflation.

**You may be experiencing lifestyle inflation if you:**

- Upgraded to a more expensive car, resulting in higher monthly payments and insurance costs, even though your previous one still works great.
- Moved to a more expensive apartment or a house without a significant need, simply because you can afford it.
- Started indulging in more costly hobbies and activities that were not part of your routine before.
- Even with a higher income, you still find yourself living paycheck to paycheck due to increased spending habits.

Houses and cars are two of the most common culprits of lifestyle inflation. In addition to the direct expense, there are often indirect or hidden costs we don't give ourselves time to factor in when rushing to get that buyer's high. Even if you can afford the higher mortgage payment of your new house, have you factored in higher property taxes, maintenance costs, and HOA fees? How does the new location impact indirectly related costs, such as increased gas expenses because you now have a longer commute to work? A more expensive car may be an important status symbol for you, but will it require you to order expensive replacement parts from Italy and exclusively use the pricier synthetic oil?

This isn't about the ability to afford these changes, but rather the long-term impact they have on our financial well-being. Sure, they seem like small and insignificant increases, but they add up extremely quickly. Five dollars here, $2 there, $10 one day, and $20 the next—it doesn't take long before these subtle and minor expenses start to put a major dent in our budgets. Over time, this inflation in spending starts to slowly steal money away from savings, investing, and debt repayment or investments that could set us up for success in the future.

Don't get me wrong, I love buying nice things and treating myself to big and small luxuries, but for a while, I overindulged at the expense of saving, investing, and building an emergency fund. So much so that in 2013, when I was living in St. Louis with my then-husband, I nearly faced a utility disconnection due to being roughly $20 short on my bill. I remember sitting at my kitchen table, faced with the consequences of my spending habits. I'd lost count of how many times I'd spent $20 on forgotten purchases over the weeks leading up to this disconnection notice. Yet it was not just about the $20. It was the fact that this wasn't an isolated incident; it was a part of my pattern of financial neglect that led me to this point. Sure, I could've reached out to my family or friends for the money, but I was filled with shame. I was embarrassed. I was embarrassed not just by the idea of having to ask someone for $20 but also by the fact that this situation was completely preventable.

Every unnecessary expense is a missed opportunity to secure our finances and creates a vulnerable position where even a small misstep can lead to a potential financial crisis. This $20 moment was a wake-up call. Your wake-up call may not be a $20 shortfall, but rest assured that if lifestyle inflation continues to go unchecked, it will manifest in one way or another, often in areas you least expect. It could be a declined card when your car is on empty and you're already running late for work, or the realization that, even though your income has increased, your savings have barely grown. These moments may not always be dramatic, but when we allow our lifestyle expenses to creep mindlessly, we're setting ourselves up for a rude awakening. We all struggle with recognizing and resisting these temptations. We don't always think about the long-term impact of our daily choices. It's human to give in to instant gratification and FOMO sometimes. We've all done it. The point is just to be more aware of our thought patterns and behaviors while cutting ourselves some slack when we mess up. So, whenever we feel the need to unnecessarily upgrade our possessions and experiences, we need to ask ourselves why and consider the long-term consequences. If this will take us further from our financial goals, is it truly what we want? Recognizing the temptation of lifestyle inflation is an essential first step in understanding our underlying money mindset.

## You Can't Outearn Lifestyle Inflation

The chances of amassing so much wealth that we literally have more money than we could ever spend in a lifetime are slim for the vast majority of us. It's much more likely that if we don't rein in lifestyle inflation early on, we'll get stuck in paycheck-to-paycheck cycles of instant gratification regardless of our income.

Making more money doesn't necessarily lead to financial stability and doesn't solve underlying issues, money mindsets, and learned behaviors. When my income first increased, I had an opportunity to continue building a solid financial foundation. My expenses were low, and I could've used that increase in funds to amplify my growth. Unfortunately, I failed to see the wealth-building potential of my low-expenses/higher-income situation. Instead, I viewed the extra money as "free" and treated it accordingly. This was the first time my wages were directly deposited into my account every week, which felt like magic. Unfortunately, the money flowed out just as quickly as it flowed in, starting what felt like a never-ending cycle. I didn't check my bank account or track my spending anymore. I knew that as long as I showed up to work, I would receive a paycheck within seven days and cover all my expenses. What harm could come from spending freely?

I thought I deserved to treat myself for putting in the work to make the money. My ability to say yes to previously unattainable luxuries or experiences first created a sense of empowerment and accomplishment, but unfortunately, those feelings were short-lived. This was the case with funds I received outside my job as well. The year after I gave birth to my first son in 2008, I got what, to me at age twenty, was a sizable tax refund for the first time. Before that, I can't remember ever having more than $1,000 in my bank account, so getting a refund of around $4,000 felt like I'd won the lottery. My initial urge wasn't to invest or save this money. I immediately wanted to purchase everything I had previously denied myself.

The only smart thing I bought was a 1999 Saturn two-door coupe for $1,800. This car immensely improved my quality of life immediately and long term. I no longer had to ask for rides, take expensive taxis, or ride the bus. The car also gave me a new sense of freedom. I no longer felt like a burden or restricted by other people's schedules. Unfortunately, I have no idea what I did with the rest of the refund I received. The problem isn't that I spent the money, but that I have no recollection of what I spent it on, meaning they were likely impulse purchases that were neither meaningful in the moment nor contributing to my long-term goals.

Living on less had required me to track expenses, budget, and live with financial discipline. Knowing my expenses would be covered by my higher income gave me much-needed mental relief while also making me believe I didn't need to maintain those healthy financial habits anymore. My higher income brought a wave of temptations, and I quickly found myself falling back into old habits, such as spending without knowing my account balance or tracking extra expenses in my budget. The truth is that you can't make the most of increased income, whether it's a higher salary or an annual or onetime cash infusion, without effective money management strategies. I kept finding myself in the same unfortunate financial situations as before, such as bouncing checks, racking up account overdraft fees, and damaging my credit score due to late payments. One time, I even had to switch banks, because the first one closed my account.

Being in financial survival mode is stressful, but getting out of that "do or die" mindset for the first time came with its own set of problems. I learned that more money itself is not a solution—it's the strategic and deliberate use of that money that determines whether we'll improve or damage our financial situation. While I stayed with my mom, I saved most of my money and felt in control of my financial future for the first time. I put my head down and focused on creating financial stability for my son. I wanted to believe that I did everything to prepare for success, but I soon realized I hadn't fully addressed my underlying money mindsets.

## Location, Location, Location— Environment Really Does Matter

It was a hard truth for me to swallow that this sense of financial stability was created in an environment free of temptations. It was one thing to practice financial discipline when I lived at home with my mom in 2008 and 2009, after the birth of my first son. She was supportive of my financial goals and allowed me to hyperfocus. She lived in the suburbs, meaning I had to drive to get anywhere, so it was much harder to make spontaneous purchases. I wasn't doing so well out in the wild, once I moved into my own apartment with help from a tax refund about halfway through 2009. I was inundated with an avalanche of enticing products and experiences while simply walking down the street and having ready access to anything I wanted. I didn't want to be the perpetually broke friend or the mom who always tells their kid no. I couldn't figure out how to balance my financial goals with living my life.

Living this contrast made me realize how much our financial experience can be shaped by the environment we live in. Understanding environmental influences is important for anyone seeking to navigate their financial journey successfully. I felt much more supported at my McDonald's job and made better financial decisions partially because of the encouraging environment, although my position at the insurance company looked more impressive on paper. I felt pressure to buy nicer clothes and attend professional networking events when I worked at the insurance company—expectations that didn't exist when I worked at McDonald's. So, while I might have looked more successful while at the insurance company, I felt McDonald's was a much more supportive environment for making good financial decisions, partially because I wasn't worried about fulfilling outside expectations.

Although we're responsible for our decisions, our surroundings have a significant impact on our money mindset, perspectives, beliefs, and how likely we are to make decisions to protect our financial well-being or cause destruction. Once we are removed from that environment, whether it was supportive or damaging, it can be difficult to navigate that change. In my case, it exposed the true extent of the financial challenges I faced.

If you grow up in a low-income community with limited job opportunities and comparably high living expenses, your financial journey may be filled with challenges to make ends meet, many of them completely out of your control. For an entire decade, I lived in an area that had only one major grocery store. When it shut down, I didn't own a car, so I had to buy food from convenience stores, instantly tripling my grocery budget.

The people we surround ourselves with can also influence our spending decisions. Most of us have that one friend or family member who's a shopaholic, accumulating possessions while struggling to pay their monthly bills. It's not about passing judgment, but we've all made these observations, and many of us know these people or have them in our lives. Although their choices are their own, they also represent real-life examples of financial choices we might want to reconsider and learn from. On the other end of the extreme, many of us also know that one person who's the opposite and places a high value on wealth and status, prioritizing money in every aspect of their life—professionally, romantically, and socially. Think Toni from *Girlfriends*. Depending on your friends' and family members' attitudes about money, you may find your own values shifting or adapting to a similar mentality, even if it's not what you actually value. It's important to remember that the financial example we're modeling for our friends and family can rub off on them, too, for better or worse.

## Practical Steps to Curb Lifestyle Inflation

My own experience of succumbing to lifestyle inflation forced me to figure out how to get back on track and prevent myself from sliding down that slippery slope over and over again. It's too easy to overlook the long-term impact that overspending can have on financial stability and our ability to achieve important life goals, such as saving for retirement, investing, or building an emergency fund.

Balancing our present desires with our future needs is a journey we all share. Sometimes giving in to lifestyle inflation without any real purpose can feel like stealing from our future selves. When we go a bit overboard on spending in our thirties, it's basically taking a few bucks from future sixty-five-year-old you. Your future self deserves security, comfort, and to enjoy all the benefits of the hard work you're putting in now. How we handle money now plays a big role in the kind of life our older selves get to kick back and enjoy. I understood this in theory, but nothing changed until I implemented these four practical steps to handle the impulse to "make more, spend more."

### 1. Recognizing Outdated Financial Beliefs and Behaviors

Financial beliefs and habits are passed down to us by our families, peers, and society. They're so deeply ingrained in us that even if we rationally understand how outdated or harmful they are, we find them lingering persistently. They don't change just because we make more money. Some of these beliefs and behaviors served us at some point, which can make them harder to give up because we may miss the familiarity. For example, if you grew up using check-cashing places, regular banks might be out of your comfort zone. If your family passed down suspicions about credit card use like mine did, you may procrastinate getting one even though it might help build your credit.

| Money Beliefs | Money Behaviors |
|---|---|
| Believing money and rich people are bad | Buying possessions you don't need |
| Believing the illusion of a perfect financial life | Satisfying others' financial expectations |
| Fearing financial uncertainties beyond your control | Attempting to control every financial aspect of your life |
| Feeling guilt and anger over past financial mistakes | Entering unhealthy financial commitments |
| Holding financial grudges | Allowing social media to trigger your FOMO, resulting in a YOLO response |
| Accepting cultural norms such as "make more money, spend more money" | Staying in your financial comfort zone |
| | Neglecting your financial health |
| | Procrastinating financial tasks and obligations |
| | Engaging in financial gossip |
| | Comparing your financial status to others |

Maybe some of these beliefs and behaviors ring true, but even if not, take the time to identify your personal money mindset and how it's impacted you. How easy is it for you to distinguish between needs and wants? Are you prone to emotional or impulsive spending? Do you respond immediately to advertising (yes, social media influencers are advertising to you)? Are you trying to fit into a certain group with "higher" financial status? What are some of the beliefs and behaviors that used to serve you but no longer fit with your current phase of life?

Recognizing these beliefs and behaviors is like pulling weeds out of a garden. Just ripping the tops off won't fix the issue—you must dig up the root cause. This requires a conscious effort on our part, and it can be difficult to acknowledge our own contributions to the financial challenges we're facing. However, it's the first step to breaking free from the cycle of reactive financial choices to proactive, intentional decisions aligned with our vision for financial well-being. Even though it's uncomfortable, questioning, identifying, and transforming the specific financial beliefs and behaviors you might have held on to for decades create the clean slate you need to set your financial goals.

## 2. Define Your Financial Goals

First, identify your three to five big-picture goals, such as buying your first home, starting a business, building an emergency fund, saving for retirement, or managing a personal investment portfolio. These goals provide the big *why* for disciplining yourself and are central to wealth building and curbing lifestyle inflation. I think of these financial life goals as the ones that require the biggest sacrifices while also contributing the most to your lifelong financial security and passing down generational wealth. Keep reminding yourself of the future rewards to avoid the temptation of instant gratification.

It's essential to base these goals on your values, not your family's opinions, what your friends are doing, or social media. If you don't care about owning a home because you want to move around, don't let your parents or the pressure of society convince you to become a homeowner because "renting is throwing away money." On the flip side, if you dream of owning investment property one day, it doesn't matter that your friends think that sounds like a big headache and they would rather put that money in the stock market. It's your goal, based on your dreams and values. You will put in the consistent effort it takes to make your goals a reality only if you choose goals that are truly important to *you*.

Once you've chosen your three to five major financial life goals, choose another three to five primary spending categories. These categories must be important enough to you that you're willing to spend extra money, even if it takes away from your major financial life goals. For me, these additional categories are a reliable vehicle because I rode public transportation with children for years, home improvements because I value a peaceful living space, and skincare because I've struggled with acne my entire life. Some of these categories may actually provide a return on investment, such as home improvements or car maintenance that could result in an increase in home value or vehicle resale value. Some of your categories may offer you an increase in confidence, peace, or comfort that's worth the expense. Others will make your life easier or buy back time to spend as you wish.

A choice *for* something always means a choice *against* something else. Because you don't have unlimited money, you have to pick major goals and additional primary spending categories. They can be flexible but must remain limited, encouraging you to create a budget that reflects your priorities. Once you've decided on these goals and spending categories, you can add line items for their related expenses to your budget.

## 3. Set a Realistic Budget

We've already talked about establishing a budget, and so has every financial expert out there, because it's a foundational piece of building wealth. However, not everyone specifically mentions adding in a buffer for inflation, due to both the economy and lifestyle creep.

Your detailed budget must be aligned with your financial goals, primary spending categories, and small luxuries in addition to your daily, monthly, and yearly expenses for necessities. I automate as many of my monthly expense payments as possible, as well as big-picture goal contributions for savings, investing, and retirement. This ensures that I avoid lifestyle inflation cutting into money set aside to cover the basics for my family and my progress toward financial goals. Because I have a cushion for discretionary spending built into my budget, I'm prepared for the times I decide to indulge in impulse buys or small luxuries. Let's not kid ourselves. We're human. It will happen, and that's okay in moderation. We can make sure we hit our larger financial goals and spare ourselves the guilt of spending a bit on ourselves by planning for these expenses.

The worksheet at the end of this chapter will help you outline these new categories and line items to incorporate into your financial planning. I've also found it a good idea to build economic inflation into my budget. Before your eyes glaze over, it doesn't have to be as complicated as it sounds. You don't need a degree in economics or understand the tedious details, but just know that the value of your money and, therefore, its purchasing power decline over time. That's what people mean when they say $100 was worth more fifty years ago than it is today.

You don't need to look up exact annual inflation rates. Let's be real. For most of my life, I had no clue what inflation was all about or how large-scale political, social, and environmental factors, such as wars, new legislation, and climate crises, impacted it. All I noticed was that my usual grocery budget didn't get me as far as it used to at the store, and clothes for my sons seemed to be getting as expensive as my own.

The Consumer Price Index (CPI) is calculated by the US Bureau of Labor Statistics and is the most widely used economic indicator of inflation. The CPI tracks price increases across major consumer expenditures—"food and beverages, housing, apparel, transportation, medical care, recreation, education and communications, and other goods and services."[1] The Federal Reserve targets an annual inflation rate of 2 percent, meaning the cost of basic goods and services shouldn't go up by more than that over the course of a year.[2] However, the actual rate has varied, especially during the COVID years, falling from a stable 1.9 percent in 2018 to 1.4 percent in 2020 before skyrocketing to 7 percent in 2021.[3] Personally, I calculate a 3

1   https://www.bls.gov/cpi/overview.htm.

2   https://www.federalreserve.gov/faqs.htm.

3   https://www.investopedia.com/inflation-rate-by-year-7253832#toc-us-inflation-rate-from-1929-to-2023.

percent economic inflation rate into my budget. If that's too much for you, don't worry, start by adding a 2 percent or even 1 percent buffer.

## 4. Resist the Urge to Overspend

I wish there was a trick or hack to immediately stop overspending, but the truth is that mindfulness is the most powerful weapon. One helpful strategy to avoid impulse purchases is to institute a cooling-off period. People generally agree that making a major financial commitment, such as taking out a mortgage or student loans, should require serious consideration. Many of us apply the same to big purchases, such as buying a car, expensive equipment for your business, or funding a home DIY project. Now take that idea and apply it whenever you want to hit the "add to cart" button.

My usual go-to splurge is gold jewelry. However, I once found myself infatuated by a particular black-and-gold Gucci purse. I saw it. I purchased it. The thrill of that purse faded before the transaction even cleared, and by the time the purse arrived it became another item to throw into my closet. I didn't purchase that purse because I *liked it*. In one Google search I could've found a hundred black-and-gold purses. I purchased that purse because it was Gucci, and I believed that was what I was supposed to do because I had the money to do it. **Wrong.** I've learned to consciously pause when I feel that urge rising. We all like to believe we make rational decisions, but buying stuff is often wrapped up in all kinds of emotional needs, so taking that cooling-off period or asking myself, "Girl, why do you need this?" allows me to:

- Consider if the item is a need or want
- Determine if the purchase contributes to my long-term financial goals
- Decide if it falls into one of my primary spending categories
- Make a conscious decision to splurge on this luxury if it fits into my discretionary budget line item
- Postpone the purchase if I'm already at my spending limit

It's up to you how to customize your cooling-off pause. Maybe you'll need a few hours, a day, or a week. You can also consider the dollar amount of your purchase, triggering a pause every time you want to buy something for more than $25, $50, or $100. You know yourself best and can adjust the specifics accordingly.

For me, another important part of resisting the urge to overspend is experimenting with decreasing my spending while increasing my income, which helps me appreciate what it takes to make those changes so I'm even less likely to jeopardize my gains. I started by challenging myself with the goal of decreasing my spending by 1 percent while simultaneously increasing my income by 1 percent. It doesn't have to be a lot, because it's more about the practice of doing it. Can I use public transportation to save on gas while picking up some overtime at work? Can I cancel that gym membership I never use and switch to a cheaper streaming service, while selling some of those items I never use on Poshmark or at an online or local marketplace? Of course, there are countless ways to accomplish this, so here are just a few options.

**Ways to decrease your expenses:**
- Leverage discounts and coupons—keep an eye out for discounts, take advantage of cashback apps and programs, and don't hesitate to use coupons when they can save you money on things you were already planning to buy.
- Buying preowned items—like furniture, electronics, or clothing—to enjoy quality goods at a fraction of the cost
- Negotiate when possible—it doesn't matter if it's a bill, a subscription service, or a large purchase; it never hurts to ask, and you'd be amazed at how often companies are willing to offer discounts to retain customers.
- Cooking at home and meal prepping rather than dining out
- Applying for social services and benefit programs

**Ways to increase your income:**

- If your current job offers the option, volunteering for extra shifts or overtime can quickly increase your earnings.
- Explore opportunities in your field that offer higher salaries or better benefits. Update your résumé, network, attend industry events to help you discover roles with better pay.
- Identify skills or hobbies that can generate some extra income on the side. Consider the things that you are already skilled in such as administrative work, freelance writing, graphic design, tutoring, or consulting.
- Declutter your home and sell clothes, toys, equipment, or electronics your family no longer uses on eBay, FB Marketplace, or Poshmark.
- Leverage your professional expertise or talents by creating digital products or courses based on your audience.

It's a great exercise to understand the reality of how much impulse spending impacts my financial life and how much effort it takes to make up for giving in to these cravings.

Practicing these four fundamental steps of recognizing outdated financial beliefs and behaviors, defining financial goals, setting a realistic budget, and resisting the urge to overspend has helped me transform automatic lifestyle inflation into intentional lifestyle design.

## Lifestyle Inflation Versus Lifestyle Design

The best thing you can do for your money is to stop trying to prove to others that you have it. Seeking external validation through material possessions leads to a never-ending cycle of trying to keep up appearances.

Trending across social media are influencers showcasing material possessions for status. Luxury is portrayed as a collection of high-end items, over-the-top vacations, and exclusive experiences instead of personal satisfaction, values alignment, and genuine fulfillment. This creates pressure to conform to these outrageous external standards of success, often at the expense of the individual's long-term financial and emotional well-being and authentic happiness. It's easy to feel left out, inadequate, and unworthy when bombarded with images of private yachts and jets, designer outfits, and VIP events.

Doing this work on preventing lifestyle inflation allows you instead to design a life that balances financial security and wealth building with creating a life of joy by spending money on experiences and things that truly matter to you. Their value is not diminished by their lack of recognition on social media or whether they fit into the most popular trends.

My concept of luxury is that it's deeply personal and subjective, way beyond material possessions or dominated by societal expectations. Defining luxury for yourself is a transformative act that disrupts this damaging trend one person at a time. Yes, it's possible to opt out of the social media rat race and focus on what truly makes you feel happy and abundant.

## Define Big and Small Luxuries for Yourself

Big luxuries are worth spending money on, even if it means having less to put toward your major goals. What adds that much to your quality of life? These bigger luxuries should match the primary spending categories in your strategic budget. If there is a mismatch here, you need to reconsider what to include in your three to five primary spending categories to account for the budget line items. For me, these are reliable transportation, home improvements, and top-of-the-line skincare. I had zero interest in buying a new car when I paid off my old one. Reliable transportation is important to me. Having a fancy car is not.

Before purchasing my current vehicle, I drove my paid-off 2013 Hyundai Elantra for years. I was perfectly happy with my car and considered it a sign of personal success and financial stability that I no longer had a monthly car payment and could invest that money for my sons. Several people tried to convince me that I should get a new car because it was their idea of success. Mine was using that money I'd saved and invested to pay an entire year's worth of tuition for my son's private school, and the fulfillment and peace that came from my ability to do that.

When you're defining luxury for yourself, pay attention to what brings you joy, even if it goes against societal norms. Maybe it's travel, an expensive hobby, personal development, or giving to community causes. Is what really matters how many likes you'll get from showcasing your "haul," or the meaningful moments you experienced while visiting your sister across the country, or the confidence you gained learning to play tennis in your thirties?

Do you care about impressing people on the internet or finding true satisfaction?

**Big luxuries often include:**
- Travel
- Vehicles
- Sports and recreational equipment
- Expensive hobbies or classes
- Coaching or mentoring programs
- Cosmetic treatments
- Home improvements or renovations

In addition to big luxuries, small luxuries matter to you personally, elevate your daily quality of life, and come with great benefits to your mood, confidence, or comfort while being relatively affordable. Small luxuries can be added to your budget as a recurring line item, for example, if you get a monthly massage. You can also designate a specific dollar amount each month for discretionary spending and use it for different things or experiences.

The value of an experience or small luxury isn't diminished by its lack of recognition on social media. Does it bring you joy?

**Small luxuries can include:**
- A nice pair of pajamas
- Consistent skincare routine
- Quality bedding to enhance your sleep
- Monthly dinners at your favorite restaurant
- Clothes and shoes that boost your confidence
- DIY projects or starting a new hobby just for fun
- Small and frequent "just because" gifts for yourself and loved ones
- Spontaneous experiences for your children

Reflecting on your personal definition of luxury beyond superficial expectations and cultural pressures will allow you to design a financial life guided by authenticity, intentionality, and the understanding that true wealth extends beyond accumulating stuff. Personal luxury is an intimate and individual process.

Who gets to decide that I need a luxury car or designer shoes, when I'm happy with my weekly bouquet of flowers for $15? I love having fresh flowers in my home because of the outsize effect they have on my mood. Arranging colorful blooms in my favorite vase to place on my coffee table in the living room makes me happier than driving a new car off the lot. I know myself, so I don't care if anyone agrees or understands my personal idea of luxury.

Letting your idea of luxury be guided by your internal desires rather than external expectations is an act of self-preservation and a declaration that your happiness, fulfillment, and financial choices are not dictated by the outside but by a deeply personal understanding of what brings richness to your life. Lifestyle design gives you the freedom of balance. This intentional approach transforms your increased income into a powerful tool for building a secure financial foundation without feeling like you're depriving yourself.

No need to be extreme and spend it all or save it all when you set unique financial goals and create a realistic budget. Soon, you'll realize that you can live a rich life that goes hand in hand with building financial wealth without blindly giving in to lifestyle inflation. Once you've done the important work of questioning your money mindset and outdated financial beliefs, you're ready to prioritize your big-picture goals and can joyfully spend money on big and small luxuries that improve your quality of life.

## Spend Smart, Live Large—How to Beat Lifestyle Inflation Worksheet

### 1. LET GO OF HARMFUL FINANCIAL BELIEFS AND BEHAVIORS.

Everyone has their own outdated or harmful financial beliefs and behaviors based on personal, familial, and societal influences, but here's a list to get you started:

- Purchasing items that don't contribute to your financial well-being
- Trying to satisfy everyone's financial expectations
- Attempting to control every financial aspect of your life
- Believing the illusion of a perfect financial journey
- Fear of financial uncertainties and factors beyond your control
- Unhealthy financial commitments
- Financial insecurities dictating your decisions
- Overindulging in social media's influence on your FOMO
- Staying in your financial comfort zone
- Neglecting your financial health and procrastinating financial tasks and obligations
- Holding financial grudges
- Comparing your finances to others'

- Engaging in financial gossip
- Guilt and anger over past financial mistakes
- Add your own
- Add your own
- Add your own . . .

## 2. DEFINE YOUR FINANCIAL GOALS AND PERSONAL LUXURIES

Write down your three to five big-picture goals, such as buying your first home, building an emergency fund, or investing for retirement.

- Add goal
- Add goal
- Add goal . . .

Write down the three to five primary categories you're willing to spend extra money on, even if it takes away from your overall financial goals (these are the big luxuries that really matter to you).

- Add big luxury
- Add big luxury
- Add big luxury . . .

Write down the small, everyday luxuries that matter in elevating your quality of life.

- Add small luxury
- Add small luxury
- Add small luxury . . .

## 3. SET A REALISTIC BUDGET

Establish a detailed budget that's aligned with your financial goals, and your big and small luxuries in addition to your daily/ monthly/yearly expenses.

- Incorporate economic inflation into your budget by adjusting your overall budget annually by a set percentage.
- Account for lifestyle inflation by adding a specific percentage on top-of-the-line items for financial goals and primary spending categories.

## 4. RESIST THE URGE TO OVERSPEND

Based on the chapter content, name your top three strategies for resisting impulse purchases:

- Add your answer
- Add your answer
- Add your answer . . .

# CHAPTER 7

# Compound Interest Is Your Best Friend (Investing)

Whenever I talk about retirement, it makes me think back to my great-grandmother, whom I called Granny. Granny was the matriarch of our family, and she worked in a cafeteria at a public school in St. Louis until she was in her sixties. My great-grandfather had passed away decades before, so it was just Granny when it came time to retire. I was in middle school at the time, so I understood only so much. What I understand now is that Granny didn't have any kind of retirement savings—401(k)s weren't a thing back then, she didn't work at a job that offered a pension (we'll get into all of this later in the chapter), and I would imagine that it felt either impossible or overwhelming to her to contemplate saving for retirement on her own. She received Social Security checks every month, but that wasn't enough to live off, so my parents, grandma, and great-aunts and -uncles provided financial assistance when necessary.

For a long time, Granny managed to live independently. She was always cooking, cleaning, and doing the laundry. Not only that, but she continued to take on a lot of responsibility that required financial contributions—a couple of my cousins lived with Granny for a while, and I lived with her for a year too. Back then, I never stopped to think about how all this must have been a financial strain, but I do remember thinking that Granny always looked exhausted, even though I never once heard her complain. I never saw her travel or do anything that looked like self-care. Instead, she was taking care of other people, even though it must have been difficult to even care for herself on that sort of limited budget.

Toward the end of her life, Granny was diagnosed with dementia. As her health started to decline in her final years, my family really stepped in. Since Granny could no longer live alone (or even take care of herself after a certain point), she moved in with various members of our family at different times. No one had the money to assume 100 percent of the responsibility, so everyone pitched in as they could, which resulted in Granny moving from place to place, without a sense of stability. Looking back on it, I feel proud of the solidarity in my family and how we all supported one another. But I also wish that it could've been different for her. Granny cracked jokes here and there, but I never really saw her laugh a lot or have fun.

I wish that Granny's life—and especially her final years—could have been freer and lighter. I wish that my family hadn't felt the financial strain of caring for her, which took a toll on everyone. As I think about my own future, Granny's situation has taught me the importance of establishing my own financial security before taking on extensive family responsibilities beyond my means. While Granny's generosity was profound, the truth of the matter is that she spent too much of her fixed income caring for other members of the family—money that she could have saved to have more options in those later years when her battle with dementia was getting worse. I think how much more comfortable Granny might have been if she'd been able to stay in her own bed, in her own comfortable home, in her own familiar space. I also think about how my family could have enjoyed those final years with Granny in a different way if they hadn't borne the responsibility of being caregivers, which is demanding and exhausting.

Witnessing Granny's circumstances had a big impact on me. As the oldest sibling, I know that if I am lucky to live a long life like Granny, I will someday be the matriarch of our family. It's important to me to make sure that I'm ready for those postretirement years; that I'm able to live in the way I want to, enjoy life, and ensure that younger family members don't bear the brunt of the financial burden of caregiving responsibilities when I reach the point I need it. It's for this reason that investing in retirement is super important for me—and no matter how young you are, I hope you'll understand why it's important for you, too, and something that you should be thinking about today. Because, as you'll see in this chapter, when it comes to investing, the most precious resource at your disposal is time.

## Barriers to Investing

What I understand now (and wish Granny had been given the tools to understand before it was too late) is that investing for the future isn't just for the wealthy white men. It isn't something to start thinking about once you reach middle age either. But up until I learned about 401(k)s, I had every reason to believe that investing was limited to a population that didn't include me because I hadn't seen my own family invest. I didn't learn about investing in school, and the media sources I consumed didn't talk to people in my demographic about the topic. Educating myself about investing in retirement accounts felt overwhelming at first. Now I'm grateful that I'm not scared to ask questions even at the risk of looking silly, or I might have given up before I even got started. The wording around it is so complicated that it feels impossible to understand.

If you take anything away from this chapter, I hope it's this: investing is a tool for building a secure future for *everyone*, and it's best to start doing so very early on in your career, even when you're saving only a little bit of money at a time. Investing is not for when you're wealthy; it's one of the important tools for building financial security in the first place.

Especially as a woman, a retirement account is not an option—it's a *necessity*. And I promise, investing in this kind of account isn't nearly as complex as you may have been led to believe. The earlier you can gain a basic understanding of why, how, and where to save for retirement, the more money you can make, the more easily you can retire, and the better quality of life Future You (and your children and grandchildren) can enjoy.

As you read this chapter, I'm asking you to shift your mindset and begin to think of investing not just as something you *can* do, but as something you *must* do. I'll show you how.

## Retirement and Women

What *is* different is the investment needs of men and women, especially when it comes to retirement. Investing in the future is even *more* important for women than men for a variety of reasons, starting with the gender pay gap. I covered some of this in chapter 1, but it's worth revisiting because it has such a major impact on our ability to build long-term wealth. As of January 2022, women earn 83 cents for every dollar earned by men working the same position (interesting fact: the United States is actually a bit behind the global average of 84 cents on the dollar).[1] The statistics are even worse for Black women, who earn between 69.5 cents for every dol-

---

1   Bureau of Labor Statistics, US Department of Labor, *The Economics Daily*, "Median Earnings for Women in 2022 were 83.0 Percent of the Median for Men." https://www.bls.gov/opub/ted/2023/median-earnings-for-women-in-2022-were-83-0-percent-of-the-median-for-men.htm (visited February 02, 2024).

lar a white, non-Hispanic man earns.[2] In addition to the pay gap, women are also far less likely to hold leadership or higher-paying roles than men. As of October 2023, women held only 37 percent of all senior management roles, with Black women holding only 10 percent of those positions. The higher up the leadership level goes, the less likely women—particularly Black women—are to attain those roles.[3] Because women earn less than men and are also less likely to advance significantly throughout the course of their career, we need to understand how to stretch our money further, not only on a day-to-day basis, but also when it comes to spreading it out and saving for our future.

There's also the fact that the latest research from the CDC shows that women have a longer life expectancy than men (seventy-nine versus seventy-three years), which means they have more time to stretch their money across. They are also more likely to be the sole living spouse and source of income. All this contributes to what's known as *longevity risk*, the risk that your life outlasts your savings.

Add all this up—lower wages, less time in the workforce, and a longer life span—and it means that women generally require more resources to comfortably retire than men do, *and* they have more of an uphill battle generating those resources. Women sixty-five and older have a median household income that is only 83 percent that of men[4]

2    Elise Gould and Katherine DeCourcy, Economic Policy Institute, *Working Economics Blog*, "Gender Wage Gap Widens Even as Low-Wage Workers See Strong Gains." https://www.epi .org/blog/gender-wage-gap-widens-even-as-low-wage-workers-see-strong-gains-women-are-paid-roughly-22-less-than-men-on-average/#:~:text=Black%20women%20are%20 paid%20only,hourly%20wage%20gap%20of%20%249.84 (visited February 2, 2024).

3    Emily Field et al., McKinsey & Company, "Women in the Workplace 2023." https://www. mckinsey.com/featured-insights/diversity-and-inclusion/women-in-the-workplace (visited February 2, 2024).

4    National Institute on Retirement Security, "Still Shortchanged: An Update on Women's Retirement Preparedness." https://www.nirsonline.org/2016/03/women-80-more-likely-to-be-impoverished-in-retirement/ (visited February 2, 2024).

and are 80 percent more likely to be impoverished in retirement than men are.[5]

But don't let this intimidate you, let it empower you. Just by being informed, you are already arming yourself with the tools needed to get ahead on your financial journey. By understanding some of the potential obstacles in your way to saving for a secure retirement, you can also begin to understand how to overcome them. Thankfully, the solution is straightforward and within reach: it's crucial that women start saving early and do so consistently, even if it's just a small contribution. For all the resources that you might *not* have earlier in your career, what you do have is time. And time, when used wisely, changes the game.

## Time Is Your Greatest Resource

Today I look back on that time I wasn't investing as time wasted. Time is one of the most powerful tools in investing, and I want every young person to know this from the minute they step into the workforce. The wonderful and powerful thing about time is that it's equitable: we've all got it, no matter how much money we're taking home, so use it to your advantage! **Time is *the* driving force of investing when income is limited.** I cannot stress this enough.

Think about it like this: Say you get your first full-time job with retirement benefits at age twenty. You start putting $100 a month into your retirement account that invests the money into stocks and bonds. The average annual rate of return for the stock market is 10 percent. Because of compound interest, over time, even small, consistent investments can grow exponentially and transform into a lot of money. After one year, you have $1,210. After five years, $7,764. Then it starts to get interesting. Compound interest is like a snowball rolling down

---

5    Jennifer Brown et al., National Institute on Retirement Security, "Shortchanged in Retirement: Continuing Challenges to Women's Financial Future." https://www.nirsonline.org/reports/stillshortchanged/ (visited February 2, 2024).

a hill, getting progressively faster and more massive. After ten years, you'll have $20,484, and after twenty years, a whopping $68,640. So, if you started at age twenty, investing only $100 a month, when you retire at sixty, you'll have $364,998.

So, don't believe the hype: some people will have you believe that if you can't save hundreds or thousands of dollars per month or max out (deposit the maximum amount allowed) your retirement account every single year, you might as well not invest at all. This is self-defeating, 100 percent false, and especially dangerous for women to buy into since compound interest can make or break our retirement experience.

But unfortunately, like me, most young people either aren't taught about investing early enough to maximize the benefit of compound interest, or we can't pull up out of the present moment enough to grasp how important it is to start somewhere—anywhere. But for every paycheck you're not investing, you're missing out on potential growth. *Start with what you have, as soon as you can.*

## How Retirement Works

As recently as the 1970s and '80s, people didn't have to save for retirement like they do today. This is because most companies offered *pensions.* You can think of a pension as a salary that continues into retirement. The amount of a pension payment varies from one person to the next and is usually based on factors like the number of years the employee worked for a company and the salary they made during their working years.

Today, pensions are largely a thing of the past, and instead employers offer retirement savings accounts, which are often referred to as 401(k)s (we'll get into these soon). Whereas pensions ensured that additional money kept coming in beyond the working years, today people have to multitask, stashing their money for retirement away during their working years so that it lasts into retirement and for the remainder of their living years. Adding to the complexity of the situation is that you don't know how long that horizon is because you can't predict your life span.

One other income source during retirement is Social Security. This government program provides financial assistance to retirees over the age of sixty-two and is funded through taxes taken out of your paycheck during your working years. The amount of Social Security you receive is calculated based on how much money you've contributed via these taxes over the course of your career. Social Security is great, but it's not without issues . . . and it's not something you should rely on to fund your retirement. First, the amount of Social Security you receive per month will almost certainly not be enough to cover all your expenses. And second, there is some concern about the longevity of the Social Security program due to changing demographics.

This means that our generation and beyond need to think about and plan for retirement in ways that generations before us did not. We need to develop a strategy to both live and save at the same time, and to stretch that savings out as far as possible into the future. And the best way to stretch that savings is to invest it . . . which is where retirement accounts come in.

## Types of Retirement Accounts

Now that you know why you should invest in your retirement, the question is: How do you do that?

There are two main categories of retirement accounts: *401(k)s*, which are only available through your employer, and *individual retirement accounts* (or IRAs), which anyone can open simply by creating an account at a financial institution (there are many, but some you've probably heard of include companies like Fidelity, Charles Schwab, J.P. Morgan, and Vanguard). You can have one or both of these types of accounts. Both 401(k)s and IRAs are long-term savings, tax-advantaged investment accounts that help you save for retirement. This means that you won't pay income taxes on the money earned that you invest in your IRA; you'll defer the tax payment until you withdraw money from the account (presumably upon retirement), which allows you to earn interest on that money in the meantime. The specifics of this depend on the type of account you have.

One thing that's important to know off the bat is that because the purpose of these accounts is to save money until retirement, although you can technically withdraw money before retirement, you'll have to pay tax on the money you take out plus a penalty fee for early withdrawal. Not to mention losing out on some of that compound interest. It's always best to avoid doing this if at all possible.

### Traditional 401(k)

I think that 401(k)s are one of the easiest ways to start investing simply because there's less to figure out based on the fact that your employer already has the account set up—all you have to do is opt in, and then decide exactly how that money is invested within your account (we'll discuss this on page 140). When you opt in to your company's 401(k) account, you agree that they can take a certain percentage or dollar amount out of every paycheck you earn and put it directly into your 401(k) account. This is another great thing about a 401(k): your savings is automated because it comes directly out of your paycheck. You're not taxed on the amount of your paycheck that goes into your 401(k) at the time your salary is paid or at the end of the tax year, so all that extra money that would have normally been taxed is instead collecting interest in your 401(k) account. You will pay taxes on the money you withdraw from your 401(k) when the time comes, though, which means it's *tax-deferred*.

Another great benefit of a 401(k)—and the reason you should always, *always* opt in, even if you're contributing a small amount—is that employers may provide a contribution in addition to your own, which is known as an *employer match*. This means that you're giving up free money by not taking part in the 401(k).

Although your employer sponsors your 401(k), it belongs to you. If you leave your job, you have the option to either roll the amount you've saved in your 401(k) into another 401(k) account with your new employer or add it into your own personal IRA. Your previous employer's contributions to your 401(k) account may or may not come with you, depending on their *vesting* policy, which is the designated amount of time after which that money officially becomes yours, whether you remain with the company or not. In some cases, you are immediately vested, and in other cases, it might happen over the course of years.

## Roth 401(k)

Not every employer offers a Roth 401(k), but some do. The difference between a Roth and a standard 401(k) account is that money deposited into your Roth is taxed along with the rest of your salary. You may be wondering why you would want to do this. Good question! Because the money is taxed *before* it goes into your account and income can be taxed only once, you will not owe any additional money when you withdraw it upon retirement (though you will incur penalties if you withdraw from this account before the age of fifty-nine and a half).

## Traditional IRA

A traditional IRA is a straightforward account in which you deposit tax-deferred income, much like you do with a 401(k). Anyone can open or contribute to an account as long as you've earned taxable income that year, and you can also do this in addition to your employer-sponsored 401(k) if you choose. The maximum contribution you can make to your traditional IRA per year is based on age (for example, the maximum amount is $7,000 in 2024 for those under fifty years old and $8,000 for those over fifty). With a few exceptions that account for extenuating circumstances, any withdrawals made before the age of 59.5 will be assessed with a 10 percent penalty in addition to the income taxes due. You must start withdrawing funds from your account (known as *required minimum distribution* or RMD) between the ages of 70.5 and 73, depending upon which rules apply to you.

### Roth IRA

A Roth IRA works like the 401(k) Roth, except it's not set up through an employer. The money you contribute is not tax-deductible; you will pay full income taxes on the money you pay into an account. That means you don't pay taxes upon withdrawal, as long as you are at least 59.5 years old and the account has been open for five years. Another benefit to Roths is that they don't have a *required minimum distribution* (RDE), like 401(k)s and other IRAs do. This means that, unlike with a traditional IRA, the investment money in your Roth can keep growing until you're ready to withdraw and use it on your own timetable.

## Investment Choices

In addition to choosing what kind of retirement account (or accounts) you want to invest your money in, you will also choose how that money is invested within the account. Retirement accounts are more than just a savings account where your money sits; the point is to grow that money over time by investing into different growth options.

As you decide what kind of assets you want to invest your money in, you'll want to consider two main factors to narrow your search: *risk tolerance* and *time horizon*. These terms might be foreign, but they refer to simple concepts.

*Risk tolerance* is how much risk you're comfortable taking with your money. Think about it like this: Some people are comfortable driving fast on the highway, even if it's riskier than driving the speed limit, because it will potentially get them to their destination more quickly. Of course, there's also the risk that they might get pulled over along the way, which could cost them time and money in the long run. For some, that risk is worth it. Other people (like me) prefer to drive the speed limit, because they prioritize getting to their destination safely without any surprises along the way, even if it takes them a bit longer to get where they're going.

*Horizon* means the length of time you can keep your money invested before you need it. There are different ways to look at this, and you have to decide what feels right to you. If you are starting to invest young and have a longer horizon until retirement, it likely means that you have more opportunity to take on risk because you also have more opportunity to recover. If you are investing later in life and have a shorter horizon, you might want to take less risk to ensure your money is there when you need it for retirement. On the other hand, you might decide to take on more risk in this scenario to potentially grow your money more quickly. *Or* you can do a bit of both . . . and this is where diversification comes in.

When your investments are *diversified*, it means that you're not putting all your eggs in one basket but spreading across different types of investments. This reduces risk, because even if one investment loses money, chances are that money you've invested in other places is still safe and growing.

With all this in mind, you can start to determine what kind of assets you want to include in your investment portfolio. You don't have to know all the answers, though—once you know your risk tolerance and horizon, you can speak with a 401(k) consultant through your HR department or at the financial institution where you opened your retirement account to help you find the best fit for your goals and situation.

### Stocks

Stocks are sold in shares, and when you invest in a share you're buying a little piece of a public company. The prices of the shares rise and fall over time, which means that your investment can either grow or decrease. Stocks are considered one of the riskier invest-ments because they are dependent on the state of a company. But if you do your research on stocks using reputable platforms such as Value Investing or AlphaResearch,[6] believe in a company and the likely growth of its industry over time, and are prepared to buy and hold your shares for at least a decade, stocks can be a profitable in-vestment option.

## Bonds

When you invest in (or buy) a bond, you're giving a company or gov-ernment a loan that they will pay back on a specific date with interest payments made along the way (usually twice a year). Bonds are lower risk than stocks because you're not riding the ups and downs of a com-pany; you're not buying a slice of the company but, instead, benefiting from interest.

## Mutual Funds

You can think about mutual funds as if you're teaming up with a group to invest in a bucket that holds a collection of stocks and bonds. The big benefit of mutual funds is diversity—not only are you getting different types of assets (stocks, bonds, etc.), but you're also investing in many different companies. It allows you to take part in the stock market without the risk that you would take on by choosing a selection of singular companies. Also, mutual funds are designed to include a collection of assets that capitalize on the overall rise of the stock market (which generally goes up over time). This makes them a good choice for those with a longer horizon because, since the market will almost certainly go up over the long run, so will your investment. Because a company is overseeing and managing mutual funds, these assets do come with a fee, which

---

6   https://www.columbia.edu/~tmd2142/5-best-stock-research-websites.html.

differs from one fund to the next, so you'll want to make sure you understand that before investing.

## Don't Wait to Invest

Even with this information, you might still be wondering how you're supposed to save for the short term and invest for the long term at the same time. Not only do you have to pay your regular expenses, but you also have to pay off debt, save money for your emergency fund and other expenses, *and* invest for retirement? I know it can feel like a lot, but I'm telling you that you *can* balance all these things at the same time.

I find it helpful to think of savings and investing as one bucket, so I have some flexibility with how much to allocate to both budget line items. In other words, I highly recommend putting some money toward both each month, but how you split up the funds depends on your short-term and long-term goals. Yes, I want to prepare for the future, but I also want to save for things that are on a shorter horizon, like maybe a new car, holiday gifts, or a vacation. The difference between these two types of savings comes down to accessibility. As you know by now, once money goes into a retirement account, it should remain there, and it's also subject to fluctuation, particularly if you've invested in assets like stocks or mutual funds. Since you'll want to access it at any given moment, money for shorter-term goals should be saved outside retirement accounts, in either a regular savings or high-yield savings account. Once you've subtracted that amount, then you can distribute the rest in your retirement account, which, by nature, won't be accessible.

What I'm telling you is that you can save for the short and long term at the same time (even if it's small amounts for both), though some financial advisers will tell you differently. For example, they might tell you to pay off all your debt so that you avoid accruing interest before you turn to investing. And yes, this might work for some people if we look at this from only a numbers perspective, but this doesn't always take into account the nuances of individual circumstances. But when building financial stability, we have to consider all the facts. Maybe you are starting to invest later, have less capital to begin with, or have a longer time line to save for than other demographics might. This is why you may not have the luxury to fully devote yourself to just one thing at a time, which matters when you're coming up with your financial game plan. When you're solely focused on paying down debt, you're potentially missing out on valuable time in the market. Investing even modest amounts early on can have a significant impact due to the power of compound interest. Delaying investing until debt is completely paid off might mean losing years of potential growth, which is very important given the longer time lines women often face when building wealth. The all-or-nothing strategy can be impractical because it assumes a level of financial flexibility that not everyone has. By integrating both debt repayment and investing into your financial strategy instead of one over the other, you can see steady progress in both areas.

However, the average consumer has over $6,000 in credit card debt at nearly 23 percent,[7] while the average investment account yields 10 percent or less in return. In other words, the credit card interest would outpace the compound interest you make on investments, racking up debt much faster than gains. In this case, paying off debt would be smarter. Ultimately, it all depends on how much debt you have, how much interest you're paying, and how much of your budget you can allocate toward paying down debt and investing. Because the best course of action depends on your specific circumstances, you may want to use an online calculator tool to plug in your information to learn whether prioritizing debt payments or investing or both simultaneously makes most sense for you.[8]

---

7   https://www.forbes.com/advisor/credit-cards/average-credit-card-debt/.

8   https://www.empower.com/learning_center/calculators/paying-debt-vs-investing.shtml#/.

## You've Got This

It took me months to save up my first $100 to invest. While that number may seem ridiculously low for some people, it was a stretch for me. When I say think small, I mean it, because that's always how I had to do it myself. Every dollar I saved toward that $100 felt like a victory. The real test was not touching the money, which I failed at multiple times. While people around me were celebrating major financial milestones like $100,000 invested, I was struggling to keep my automations going and constantly fighting the urge to withdraw my savings for more immediate needs. But I stayed committed, reminded myself why I started, and held on to the future when I would be able to celebrate a bigger milestone. When I finally saw that $100 mark in my investment account, it was more than just a number. It was a symbol of my ability to prioritize my future.

What's most important in this moment is that you start investing what you can, even if it doesn't feel like a lot of money, so that compound interest can begin doing its work for you. Small, regular investments are the key to beginning to save for your future. Even if your balance feels insignificant in the moment, don't underestimate how it can and will grow over time and how deeply that will impact not only your future but also that of those you love. You are building freedom and peace of mind. You are putting the pieces in place to begin creating generational wealth by ensuring that you can take care of yourself in your later years so that your children and grandchildren are able to begin building their own solid foundation as early as possible. When you think about it like that, you can see how investing for retirement is about more than just retirement and more than just you—it represents exponential growth for your entire family.

Also know that investment is not one and done. You'll want to reevaluate your finances on a regular basis as your earnings and life circumstances change, then adjust your investment contributions as you can. Sometimes you will be able to save more, and other times you might be in a situation where you can save less; again, we're going for consistency above all else.

Because you're in this for the long haul, it's important to celebrate the progress you make along the way! *This is a long-term project, and the payoff won't come for years.* So, remember to celebrate yourself for incremental movements toward your savings goals because it's a big deal. Instead of focusing on achieving big numbers (which can be intimidating), concentrate on the milestones, such as saving your first $100, making your first investment, or reaching a monthly savings goal.

Finally, I want to be clear that I'm not saying this is easy. It's not, and especially in those moments when tough decisions are involved and you feel like your money is already stretched to get you through this week, let alone into the future. Making the right financial decisions doesn't always feel good in the moment! It can leave you feeling uncomfortable, sad, and angry—even when you know that decision is for the best. If you find yourself in a situation like this, know that none of these feelings mean you made a wrong decision, just that you made a tough one. Those are two very different things. When you feel the weight of a financial decision, remind yourself that it's often through these tough choices that you're making your life easier in the future and can have a different set of options before you in the long run.

I find it helpful to think of savings as health care. Much like I might sometimes prefer to eat fries instead of a smoothie, I know that over the long run I'm going to feel better if I make the decision that helps me stay the healthiest. (Also, sometimes you just want to eat those fries—and you *should* treat yourself.) Saving money isn't the absence of spending money. It's about being intentional with how you allocate that money and making sure that some of it goes toward your future.

I promise, you'll be glad you did.

# CHAPTER 8

# Closing the Gap (Credit)

One rainy morning in 2017, I was waiting at a bus stop on the south side of St. Louis with my sons, who were nine and five at the time, when a passing car drove through a puddle and completely drenched me with muddy water. Immediately, I felt the tears well up in my eyes while I fought the urge to turn around and go back home. But without a car, there was no way I would've made it back home to change into clean clothes, drop off my sons at day care, and still get to work on time. My options were going to work with dirty, wet clothes, hoping they'd dry on the way to give me back an ounce of dignity, or calling out of work and missing a full day's pay. I chose to go to work, realizing I didn't have the time or money to fix even a small, accidental inconvenience.

Standing there soaked and wet, I couldn't help but face my harsh reality; my financial situation stripped away my ability to respond to unpredictable moments, and without a safety net or lifeline, every minor mishap could escalate to a financial crisis in a matter of minutes. This also highlighted a deeper issue—the lack of a financial buffer or alternative when I had immediate needs but could not pay for them in full. Without any alternatives, I was always going to be one step or splash away from a setback that could derail my entire financial plan.

Credit, a luxury for some but a lifeline for many, would've been an immediate solution to getting my children and me off the bus and into safe and reliable transportation.

Instead, I felt stuck in a constant cycle. I couldn't afford to pay for a reliable car in cash because most of my money was exhausted from day-to-day expenses. I didn't know how to leverage my credit score to finance a car and make payments on it, which were equal to my monthly costs for public transportation.

## What Is Credit?

Credit is the ability to borrow money with the promise to pay it back later, often with interest. This includes credit cards, mortgages, car loans, and personal loans. Your credit score is a number that tells banks and lenders the chances of you paying them back. What we often get wrong about credit is that it can be a lifeline or a liability, depending on how well we understand it, manage it, and leverage it to close the gap and build wealth.

Unfortunately, there is some cultural shame around "bad credit." A credit score doesn't always tell the whole story. The reasons for bad credit are varied, from the most obvious of just being young and having no credit history to financial hardship such as job loss or illness, divorce, and identity theft.

## What Is a Credit Score?

Your credit score is a number representing your creditworthiness. In other words, the higher your score, the more confidence lenders like mortgage companies and car loan servicers have that you will pay back the loan.

Your credit score is made up of several factors, including the length of your credit history, your payment history (missed or late payments), the amount of debt you owe, how much debt you have in comparison to your income, the types of credit you use (installment, revolving, open), and any recent credit inquiries (checks on your credit score when you apply for loans or cards).

## What's the Difference Between a Credit Score and a FICO Score?

There are three major credit reporting companies (Equifax, Experian, and TransUnion) that all calculate credit scores and create credit reports. The Fair Isaac Corporation (FICO) was the first to calculate scores in the late 1980s in response to a need for an industry-wide standard.

Today, FICO is the most widely used credit score most lenders base their decisions on. FICO takes all the data from the three credit reporting bureaus plus information from other sources to calculate their comprehensive scores.[1] You can have a FICO score between 300 and 850. The higher, the better.

| Category | Credit Score Range |
|---|---|
| *Poor* | 300–579 |
| *Fair* | 580–669 |
| *Good* | 670–739 |
| *Very good* | 740–799 |
| *Exceptional* | 800–850 |

---

1   https://www.fico.com/independent/independence#:~:text=FICO%20is%20the%20
independent%20standard,%2D%2D%20Equifax%2C%20Experian%20and%20
TransUnion.

## Learning from Our Family's "Credit History"

Growing up, I saw my grandmother purchase essential appliances, like a fridge, and basic furniture from Rent-A-Center. She took these items home without having to pay in full, which seemed like the best option for someone with limited financial resources and immediate needs. I quickly learned about the downsides, though, when my grandma told us not to answer the phone when the company called to check on monthly payments and not to answer the door, in case they'd come by the house to collect the money or leave with my grandma's couch. She always made her payments, but the anxiety surrounding these interactions left a lasting impression on me and played a major role in my conviction that credit was bad. I figured I should stay away from credit in all forms to avoid going into debt and be harassed by bill collectors. I only ever heard about the liability side of the credit coin, never about the potential benefits.

Conversations about credit in my family were rare, and when the topic did come up, my family members spoke only of the negative aspects, such as going into debt, getting hounded by debt collectors, and struggling to pay off debt. Being in debt was regarded as a shameful, moral failure that required you to put everything behind getting out of debt as fast as possible. I wish these conversations could have been more balanced and educational, less emotional and fear-based. I would've loved to hear about the importance of using credit responsibly to build financial stability, for example, to get reliable transportation. I needed my family to discuss and model how to build and maintain good credit, by following a budget to make payments on time and explaining how to review cardholder agreements and choose a credit card based on interest rates, terms, and fees. I would have liked to learn how credit cards are an important aspect of establishing good credit and creditworthiness, and how this would affect the type of loans I could get to buy a house or finance an education.

Media representations of credit weren't exactly helpful either. Growing up in the nineties, anytime credit cards were mentioned on a TV show or movie, the storylines were predictable. It was always the wives or daughters excessively shopping and bragging about charging their purchases to their husbands' or dads' credit cards. Cue the stressed husband or dad looking at pages and pages of credit card bills, blaming their wives and daughters for making them work so hard to provide their lavish lifestyle. Another trope was a Black family somehow getting approved for a line of credit, and it quickly becoming such an important lifeline that it felt more like a joke than an honest exploration of the historically unequal access to credit.

This is a huge problem because credit doesn't affect just whether you get approved for a credit card; it influences your access to housing, transportation, and employment opportunities. Your creditworthiness determines if you're approved for a mortgage, but many property management agencies also pull your credit when you apply for a rental. The same goes for transportation, if you want to move from the bus to your own vehicle like I did. There are some dealerships that specialize in selling to people with bad credit or no credit, but these contracts usually have terrible terms, including high interest rates. An unfavorable credit history can even mess with your job prospects because many employers check their applicants' credit history, especially for roles involving financial management.

A lack of understanding and education about credit impacts almost every area of your life and keeps you stuck in a cycle of high-cost borrowing and financial instability. My beliefs about credit were so deeply ingrained in me that I had to do a lot of work on myself to dismantle them and see credit as a tool to be used responsibly and with full awareness of its benefits and dangers.

| Benefits of Credit | Dangers of Credit |
|---|---|
| Save cash | Mistakenly view it as "free money" |
| Make larger purchases (car) | Use for lifestyle inflation |
| Build wealth (buy home) | Overspend and get trapped in debt cycle |
| Get perks (travel, discounts, cashback) | |

Even as an adult and knowing much more about personal finance than I used to, I'm still struggling to overcome those old stories passed down over generations. Don't judge yourself if it's the same for you. Credit cards continue to be an area of personal finance that I tend to shy away from. While there are a ton of benefits, such as building good credit necessary for home or vehicle purchases, better fraud protection than debit cards, and perks for travel, insurance, or entertainment, I still find myself fearful of using credit cards. That's why I have only a modest amount of available credit. My credit score is strong enough to get access to much more, but it's my personal comfort zone. I say this to reassure you that it can take a while to get comfortable with using credit for your benefit. That's okay.

We'll talk through the fundamentals first so you can get an idea of how the system works and how you can use it to build wealth.

## Why the Credit Conversation Is Different for Women

Credit is incredibly important for women to understand and leverage due to historical inequality and women's need to bridge the gap of persisting wage discrimination.

### Historical Inequality

Until the Equal Opportunity Credit Act of 1974, women couldn't even get a credit card without a male cosigner, regardless of their income, creditworthiness, or previously established financial relationship with the bank. Can you imagine that only a little more than fifty years ago, you would have had to convince your dad or husband that you weren't as clueless about money as patriarchal society believed, and that you could be trusted to handle money and credit responsibly?

The Equal Opportunity Credit Act made it illegal to discriminate against applicants based on gender, race, marital status, religion, or national origin. It was an important step forward for women who could now build their own credit history, which is important for accomplishing many financial milestones that improve your quality of life and allow you to build wealth, such as renting a place, buying a car, purchasing your first home, or starting a business.

Even after the law passed, women still faced barriers, such as receiving smaller loans compared to men with the same income and credit scores. Women-owned businesses receive less financing from financial institutions. They ask for smaller loan amounts to begin with, and they also receive a smaller percentage of the requested amount than their male counterparts.[2] On top of that, according to research by Federal Reserve banks, Black-owned businesses are "significantly less likely than white-owned start-ups to receive funding through financial institutions or lenders," despite applying at similar or higher rates.[3]

## Bridging the Gap

It's true that society is moving in the right direction, but women, especially Black women, are still dealing with a wealth gap due to wage disparities, unequal access to education, credit and loans, and shouldering more unpaid and invisible labor. As I mentioned, women also bear the financial brunt of separation or divorce, experiencing a 41 percent decline in income and assets on average, nearly twice as big

2    https://www.forbes.com/sites/forbesfinancecouncil/2020/01/23/three-ways-to-close-the-business-loan-gender-gap-for-good/?sh=35d23dff11f3.

3    https://www.fedsmallbusiness.org/reports/survey/2023/2023-report-on-startup-firms-owned-by-people-of-color.

as the average decline for men.[4] Almost a third of women fall into poverty after their divorce.[5]

Credit can provide women with the means to cover necessities in temporary emergency situations, bridge the gap due to wage disparities, and increase independence by investing in education or starting a business. Of course, it's a bad idea to use credit to cover basic living expenses over long periods of time, but we don't talk enough about credit being a safety net during times of distress when you have to make immediate moves or can't rely on a spouse or family members. A credit card will guarantee access to funds when you need them most.

With all that going on, building wealth can feel overwhelming. That's why it's important to learn how to leverage credit so it can act as a basic tool to financial independence and can help you bridge the gap between systemic inequalities and your day-to-day expenses as well as your long-term financial future.

## So, How Do You Build Credit?

It's key to start small. I know I keep saying this throughout this book, and I stand by it. I'm all about making manageable changes that fit into your current life and support your personal goals. Starting with just one or two things to focus on will help you feel in control and prevent overwhelm. As you get more confident building a positive credit history, you can add on.

Now that we've dismantled some of the discomfort and shame around the credit conversation, let's dive into what you can actually do to build or improve your credit.

**Check your credit report for free at least once annually by going to www.annualcreditreport.com.**

---

4    https://www.gao.gov/assets/gao-20-541.pdf.

5    https://www.iser.essex.ac.uk/research/publications/working-papers/iser/2014-30.

## What's Included in Your Report?

So much information! Your credit report lists any credit cards or loans you received with the total credit limit or loan amount for each, a list of payment transactions, and whether the payments were on time, missed, or late.

You'll also find data for all the businesses and lenders that have obtained your report within a certain time period, your current and former names, addresses, phone numbers, and employers, as well as any bankruptcies.

## What Should You Look For?

Check your report for credit cards or lines of credit you don't recognize, addresses where you have never lived, delinquent accounts that don't belong to you, or names of employers you've never worked for. In short, look for any indication that someone is using your name or SSN to open credit lines or obtain services and committing fraud. If you find anything, go through the process to dispute these items.

## What Are the Most Common Errors?

The Consumer Financial Protection Bureau[6] advises to look for three main categories:

- *Identity errors* (wrong names, phone numbers, addresses, accounts belonging to someone with a similar name, or incorrect accounts from identity theft).
- *Account errors* (closed accounts reported as open, accounts incorrectly labeled as late or delinquent, same debts listed more than once, incorrect dates for payments or account opening).
- *Data management errors* (accounts with an incorrect current balance or an incorrect credit limit).

---

6    https://www.consumerfinance.gov/ask-cfpb/what-are-common-credit-report-errors-that-i-should-look-for-on-my-credit-report-en-313/.

## What Types of Credit Do I Use for What?

There is secured and unsecured credit, and you'll likely use both in your wealth-building journey.

**Secured credit** refers to any credit guaranteed by collateral, such as your car loan or mortgage. If you don't pay back the loan, the bank can repossess your car or take your house. These types of loans are usually big lump sums that the lender pays straight to the mortgage company or car loan servicer, and then you pay them back every month over several years or decades.

**Unsecured credit** refers to loans not guaranteed by collateral, such as student loans, personal loans, or most credit cards. Some credit cards, like the first one I ever got, are secured, meaning you have to make a deposit to open the card or link it to your bank account, so the lender can take your money if you don't make payments on time.

A secured credit card may be your only option when you first start building your credit history, and it can work well if you know how to use it and don't go into it blindly like I did. The key is to use as little credit as possible, and always pay your balance off in full and on time.

Beyond the secured and unsecured credit categories, there are several different types of credit you must know about to leverage each for the most benefit.

| | Revolving Credit | Installment Credit | Open Credit |
|---|---|---|---|
| *Examples* | Credit cards, store cards, home equity lines of credit (HELOC), personal or small business loans or lines of credit | Car loans, student loans, mortgages | Utility bills, charge cards |
| *Credit Limit* | Yes | Yes | No |
| *Payment Amount* | Flexible | Fixed | Flexible |
| *Interest / Fees* | Yes | Yes | No |
| *Repayment Terms* | Flexible | Fixed | Flexible |

I've come a long way from being completely unaware of how to improve and leverage my credit score and learning about different types of credit to financing a car. Back then, I had to wake up at 4 a.m. to catch the bus to drop off my sons at day care by 5 a.m. and get back on the bus by 6 a.m., only to make it to work by 7 a.m. On rare occasions, I splurged on a taxi or sometimes got a ride home from a kind coworker. Leveraging credit to finally finance my own car took me a long time, but it was worth it when I think back on all the sleep we missed, the dangerous situations we sometimes found ourselves in, and the constant inconveniences like missing the bus or waiting outside in the rain and snow.

The first time I tried to get car financing, I was denied because I didn't have a good enough credit history. I wish I'd known about some of these strategies to build credit quicker.

## Credit Strategies for Starters

You're not alone if, in the past, you've severely underestimated the impact of late payments, high credit utilization, or delinquent accounts.

Payment history is the most significant aspect of your credit score because it shows that you can pay back what you borrowed. It makes sense to focus on this when you're starting out, and there are several strategies specific to creating a payment history of on-time payments to increase your score:

**BECOME AN AUTHORIZED USER ON A SPOUSE'S CREDIT CARD.**

- The benefits of being an authorized user are that you don't have to get approved for your own card, and you can build credit with the help of someone else. In other words, their good credit history affects yours too. This is also an option if you're a parent and want to help your child get started building credit.

**IF YOU CAN QUALIFY FOR YOUR OWN CREDIT CARD, START WITH A LOW-COST, LOW-INTEREST-RATE, SECURED CREDIT CARD.**

- These cards are a great starter option because the credit limits are reasonable and interest rates are usually low. These cards are best used regularly without ever maxing them out. Try to stay below 30 percent of your credit limit and pay off the entire balance every month.

**CONSIDER CREDIT BUILDER LOANS.**

- Credit builder loans allow you to take on a small amount of debt (usually up to $1,000) for the purpose of demonstrating that you will make payments on time and are reliable. They are different from traditional loans in that you don't receive the actual loan amount up front. The financial institution deposits the loan amount into a savings account and releases the funds only once you have made all the payments.
- You're making monthly payments until you have met the loan amount, at which time it will be disbursed to you. In that sense, it's not really a loan because you're not getting any money until you've saved up that money yourself. This is why it's called a credit builder loan, but it won't do you any good if you need the money right now.

**PAY BILLS ON TIME BY SETTING UP AUTOMATIC PAYMENTS AND/ OR BILL PAYMENT REMINDERS.**

- Whether we're talking about credit cards or installment payments, you can set up automatic bank drafts or cell phone reminders to ensure you're never late or miss a payment. Even utility companies report to credit bureaus, so the sooner you can get all your bill paying on track, the quicker your credit score will improve.

**FOCUS ON LOW CREDIT UTILIZATION TO ENSURE FULL, TIMELY PAYMENTS.**

- You can hurt your credit score if you max out your cards, but you'll also damage it if you don't use your cards at all. Credit utilization means how much of your credit limit is currently being used. What's your credit card balance compared to your overall credit limit? Generally, the industry advice is to use 30 percent or less of your credit limit at any given time or as low as 10 percent if you're shooting for excellent credit.

- You already know how I feel about this. Sometimes, it's simply not possible to use that little because we're using credit to bridge the gap. As with all my advice, do the best you can in your current circumstances. My recommendation is to focus as much as possible on borrowing only what you absolutely need and making sure your monthly payments to wipe out your balance are calculated into your budget.

## Leveraging Credit to Build Wealth

Once you've established your credit history and score by using the starter strategies above, it's time to level up. This is where it gets fun! You'll learn how to use credit to improve your quality of life, invest strategically in your education or business, and build overall wealth. Making decisions based on improving your quality of life is a conscious choice aligned with your values and priorities, rather than blindly following societal expectations, peer pressure, and FOMO into lifestyle inflation.

### Quality of Life

Better credit allows you to apply for better rental housing since property management agencies often pull your credit and will now be less likely to deny your application based on a bad score or nonexistent credit history.

There are always exceptions, but generally you can try to get an auto loan once you have a credit score of at least 600. Most car loans with decent interest rates and monthly payments go to borrowers with higher scores; usually the upper end of the "fair" rating and above. If you are in a similar situation to mine where getting reliable transportation was more financially responsible than using public transit, this would make a lot of sense.

Quality of life extends to many aspects when credit isn't about making impulse purchases but investing in yourself, your education or career, taking a break from work while taking care of yourself, your family members, or supplementing your maternity leave. By now, you've considered how your personal values and financial priorities relate to everything from budgeting to banking, saving to investing. Now it's time to apply the same to credit, which can provide a cushion of flexibility and stability when you need it. But most importantly, credit can improve your quality of life and support you in taking steps toward major life goals.

## Homeownership

One of the most prominent goals across the board is purchasing a home, not just because it's a dream for many of us to have stable housing to call our own but also because real estate is a great wealth-building investment. With a purchase that big, your credit score matters a lot for the types of loans you can qualify for and how advantageous the terms are when it comes to interest and fees. A fraction of a percent can make a huge difference in a purchase for hundreds of thousands of dollars.

Although you can get a home loan with a credit score as low as 500, most home lenders require a credit score of 620, and the higher your score, the better your interest rates and terms. A First-Time Homebuyers (FHA) loan requires a minimum credit score of 580, while it's 640 for a Veterans Affairs (VA) loan and a minimum of 620 for conventional loans.

If you're buying a home with a partner or spouse, your two credit scores will be averaged out, which is why it matters that you and your partner are on the same page when it comes to financial goals.

## Strategic Borrowing

Strategic borrowing is taking on debt with the knowledge that it is highly likely to generate a return for you that's more than the original debt. This can apply in different scenarios, for example, taking out student loans for a degree that is in such high demand with high entry-level salaries that it will pay for itself. Another example is purchasing a rental property by applying for another mortgage, as long as you know your local rental market and have determined that your rental income will cover mortgage payments, property maintenance, and taxes while also making you a profit. Strategic borrowing can also apply if you want to start a business or are already running one.

## Business Start-Up and Expansion

In my work, I've come across many women who use credit cards or lines of credit to start or expand their businesses. Initially, you may need those extra funds to cover your loss of income once you leave your nine-to-five.

Of course, a decision to become a business owner requires a lot of planning and understanding of the risks involved. Ideally, the planning stage will include saving up for this period of financial instability. However, credit will likely be a safety net for unexpected costs or delays in getting your business up and running. If you're an established business owner, you may apply for a business loan or line of credit to expand into a second location because your market research shows that the expansion will significantly increase your revenue.

While all these strategies help you develop your credit history, improve your credit score, and build wealth by leveraging your growing creditworthiness, be patient with yourself as you unlearn old beliefs.

Most of my friends grew up in inner-city, single-parent households with low income, just like me. Our experiences with money had been very similar, and our access to educational and financial resources was limited. Like our parents, we were just trying to survive with the resources we had. It's normal to be anxious about credit when all your past experiences have been negative, and it's brave to educate yourself anyway and learn how to leverage credit for your benefit and to teach the next generation a new way.

## End-of-Chapter Checklist— How to Build/Fix/Maintain Credit
### Credit Checklist

1. Reflect on outdated beliefs about credit and reframe those old stories.

2. Check your credit report for free at least once annually by going to www.annualcreditreport.com. Check it for credit cards or lines of credit you don't recognize, addresses where you have never lived, delinquent accounts that don't belong to you, or names of employers you've never worked for. In short, any indication that someone is using your name or SSN to open credit lines or obtain services and committing fraud. If you find anything, go through their process to dispute these items.

3. Credit score monitoring. A number of paid services allow you to access your FICO score, but many credit cards also provide you with a credit score for free, which is not your official FICO score but gives you a good idea.

4. Use credit-building strategies focusing on creating a good payment history, such as becoming an authorized user, applying for

a secured card or credit builder loan, and prioritizing low credit utilization.

5.  Use wealth-building strategies to leverage credit for educational goals, business expansion, real estate purchases, and strategic borrowing.

# CHAPTER 9

# In Deep $$$$
## (Debt Management)

"What's the price of a broken heart, and how much are you willing to pay to fix it?" I was willing to pay $20,000 to fix mine, and it landed me in a cycle of deep debt for years. As a newly single mom, I was walking home from the bus stop one day when I received a call from a debt collector regarding one of the payday loans I had defaulted on. The representative told me I had to resolve the payday loan immediately, or a police officer would be dispatched to my home to arrest me. At the time, I didn't know if that threat was legitimate or even legal. It wasn't. Debt collectors have neither the right nor the power to arrest you and are forbidden by law to threaten or harass you.[1]

The interaction scared me into paying that loan in full with money I truly did not have to spare. I had to quickly figure out how to recover

1   https://www.consumerfinance.gov/ask-cfpb/can-i-be-arrested-for-an-unpaid-debt-en-1537/.

the funds that I was now lacking to pay my other bills. I was in that gray area postseparation predivorce. It was a time when I took inventory of my financial life without knowing what the future would bring and without the financial safety of court-ordered child support, custody arrangements, or a final split of assets and liabilities. Between the day the divorce was initiated and the day it was finalized, almost two years of financial instability ensued that had me racking up $20,000 in debt.

I knew that I needed to get a handle on my debt, but I felt stuck on figuring out *how*. It's easy to believe that if we just make more money, then all our financial problems will disappear, but after helping more than eighty thousand people kick-start their financial journey, I know that it's not that simple. When you need immediate financial relief, but your income is limited, and your credit is less than favorable, it's easy to fall prey to predatory practices. Especially payday loans.

Many of the obstacles we encounter around our money aren't necessarily about making more money as much as they are about having the knowledge to manage our money to avoid falling into the financial traps we've discussed throughout this book. One of these traps is taking on high-interest credit that quickly turns into overwhelming debt. That's where I found myself, and I needed a way out. I was already spread thin, so working a ton of overtime with two small children was not an available option. So I asked myself, "What can I cut back on?" I had to be realistic. I was not going to have a debt freedom story with a clickbait-y headline like "Single Mom Pays off Five-Figure Debt in Three Months." My income, caretaking responsibilities, and life circumstances as a newly single mom made that nearly impossible. I had to figure out a manageable pace to make progress on my debt. But things got worse before they got better.

## Unpopular Truth—Sometimes Debt Is Unavoidable

I know my opinion is controversial, but as I explained in chapter 8, sometimes living off borrowed money and thereby accumulating debt isn't something you can't avoid, especially when you fall into the low-income bracket or are dealing with an emergency situation. After my divorce, I was working a full-time mid-level position in default mortgage banking, making $16 per hour. I spent eight hours each day, five days a week, assisting families with their financial hardships while secretly going through one of my own. My household expenses were roughly $2,000 per month. After taxes and deductions, I had little to nothing left beyond covering our basic bills but was now faced with lawyer fees and lost wages due to court appearances in my divorce and custody case. It didn't take long before I lived paycheck to paycheck and found myself behind on bills regularly.

I learned from one of my coworkers that the local bank offered a feature that allowed me to withdraw up to $500 on an upcoming paycheck and automatically pay it back on the day my paycheck was deposited into my bank account. I used the cash advance to pay the electricity bill, but when my paycheck was deposited into my bank account and it was time to repay the money, I realized that I couldn't afford to pay that money back and also pay my rent on time.

What was I to do? I took out another loan with a payday loan company to supplement the money automatically deducted from my paycheck from the cash advance. I nervously stood in line, surrounded by a dozen other people who looked just as anxious. When it was my turn, I handed over my ID and a copy of my paycheck stub to request a $500 loan against my next paycheck. The loan came with an interest rate of 400 percent.

And so, my personal debt cycle began. At one point, I had three different payday loans and one cash advance open. I used one payday loan to pay off another and immediately took out the next one, forever trying to catch up. When payday loans were no longer enough, I started using credit cards to cover my utility payments and the payday loans to pay my rent. I struggled to pay the balances back in full, but I always remained hopeful that things would improve financially. Yet my credit card and payday loan debt were growing by the week. While

I knew I owed an overwhelming amount of money, I knew very little about debt.

## What Is Debt?

Debt is money you owe. The moment you borrow money for a purchase or use a service or line of credit with a promise to pay later, debt is created. Prior to taking out my first $500 payday loan when I was eighteen, I'd borrowed only small amounts of money—$20 for gas here or $15 for lunch there—so it was difficult for me to process the idea of owing thousands of dollars at once. I thought that the only way a person could end up owing that much money had to be a result of poor money management. I was wrong. Over 77 percent of American households are impacted by debt of some kind,[2] and that number continues to rise. Debt is common, and because wages have not kept up with the cost of living, more people depend on debt to cover their day-to-day living expenses.

In chapter 8, I shared my perspective that while taking on debt through credit lines, cards, and loans is complicated, it can be a useful tool to build long-term wealth and stability. I shared the example of taking on debt in the form of a car loan, which saved me money on transportation costs. However, this chapter focuses on how to best manage debt that's become overwhelming or threatens our financial safety and stability.

First, it's important to understand that there are several different kinds of debt that all come with different repayment terms and conditions. All debt is not created equal, and how you manage it depends on the type of debt you have.

## Types of Debt

Debt generally falls into one of four main (although sometimes overlapping) categories: secured, unsecured, revolving, and installment.

---

2   https://www.federalreserve.gov/publications/files/scf20.pdf.

**Secured debt** is debt backed by an asset. This means that an asset such as a car or house will be used as collateral for a loan, and failure to repay the loan will result in the lender taking the asset back, for example repossessing the car or foreclosing on a house due to non-payment. A secured credit card works just like a standard credit card. You can pay for purchases and choose to pay the minimum payment at the end of the month, fork over the entire balance, or pay an odd amount in between.

However, secured credit cards differ from standard credit cards in that you must send a deposit to the creditor before being granted an account. This deposit acts as collateral to the creditor and assures them that you'll be less likely to default on your payments.

The amount of money you put down as collateral is the amount that your credit limit will be. Therefore, if you place an $800 deposit, your credit limit will be $800. If you put in a $350 deposit, your credit limit will be $350. Over time, if you'd like to increase your credit limit, you do so by putting down an additional deposit. However, with a proven track record of on-time payments and responsible use, you may be granted a credit increase without the need to place an additional deposit.

**Unsecured debt** is the opposite of secured debt. It is not backed by an asset, and failure to repay the unsecured debt, such as credit cards, as agreed will result in aggressive collection practices that can lead to you being sued or your wages garnished for nonpayment. A typical credit card is an example of an unsecured debt. When you apply for an unsecured card, you aren't offering assets or making a down payment as collateral to ensure that you're "good for the money." Your approval, or lack thereof, for an unsecured card depends on your credit score and credit history.

An unsecured credit card requires no initial out-of-pocket expense to attain your credit card. But don't be surprised if fees charged by your creditor have already used a percentage of your limit.

**Installment debt** is a fixed amount paid by a borrower over an

agreed amount of time with a set number of payments. Each installment payment made lowers your original balance but also includes
interest. Installment debt or an installment loan are typically given as
one large lump sum and are usually used to purchase big-ticket items
such as a house or car.

Revolving debt or revolving credit is different from installment debt
because there is no set amount of payment. Revolving debt allows you to
borrow against an approved line of credit with the expectation that it will
be paid back. You can borrow against this debt as often as you need to,
and you are not obligated to pay off your balance each month. The most
common example of this is a credit card, but home equity lines of credit
also fall into this category, as well as personal or business lines of credit.

None of these types of debt are necessarily bad, but it's important
to know the fine print to make the best possible decision for any debt
you're considering taking on. In addition to managing your significant debts like car loans, mortgages, or personal loans, you have to
become aware of your seemingly insignificant day-to-day behaviors
that also add to your overall debt or reduce your ability to pay off
existing debt.

I spent so much time analyzing how to take money from one bill to
pay another bill that the overthinking kept me from taking any action
at all. By the time I built up the nerve to do anything, I was paying a
higher price because interest had accumulated, or I was charged a late
fee. Much of my monthly income was wrapped up in overdraft fees or
paying extra interest on my credit card bills because I didn't pay the
balance in full or on time.

Here's what you can do to stop the frantic debt cycle and start
making real progress.

## Taking Control of Your Debt

I fell into the habit of panicking about all the bills I couldn't pay while
feeling paralyzed at the same time. I learned the hard way that al-

though I could go at my own pace, I did have to take consistent action to reduce and eventually eliminate the debt I accumulated.

## Identify Your Debt

Keeping track of all your debts can be a tedious process, and believe it or not, people sometimes discover debts they were unaware of for reasons like lost mail, miscommunications, or inaccurate reporting information. Here are a few things that you need to know:

**Who and how much.** This is the name of the company or person you owe money to and the amount. For example, the specific credit card (VISA, MC, Discover, AmEx) and the exact dollar amount you owe.

**Minimum payment due.** This is the minimum payment you need to make on each debt every month to avoid any late fees or further debt collection attempts.

**Interest rate.** This is the money your creditor makes on the back end of the money they loaned you up front, by charging an extra amount for the time it takes you to pay back the debt.

**Due date.** This is the date by which payments must be made to the lender.

## Review Your Credit Report

As we discussed in chapter 8, one of the easiest ways to identify any debts you owe is to review your credit report. When a debt has been sent to a collection agency, the chances of this delinquent account being reported to a credit bureau and negatively impacting your credit are high.

## Monitor Bill Statements for Accuracy

I used to go weeks, sometimes months, without opening and reading my mail. I was stuck in a state of denial. In my mind, I believed that if I didn't open the mail or see the bill, then it didn't really exist, and I had more time to pay the bill when I was ready. I was reminded to open the mail when I could tell it was a disconnection notice only because I could see the pink paper through the white envelope. Not only was this not a good practice, but I also didn't give myself a chance to review my statements to determine if I'd been appropriately charged.

For over a year, I complained that my cell phone bill was too high. I spent most of my cell phone bill due dates calling and making payment arrangements and trying to stretch the unpaid balance out for weeks to give me more time to pay it off. One day, out of curiosity, I sat down and looked over my cell phone bill, and to my surprise, for over a year, I'd been charged for a cell phone that I never owned. Turns out, the representative made an error and added monthly installment payments for a brand-new cell phone instead of the much cheaper device I purchased in full at the time I signed up for my services. I don't think this was done intentionally. I bought my phone around Christmas, one of the busiest times of the year, but this error was costing me hundreds of dollars. Once I realized the error and alerted the phone company, the money was added as a credit to my account, but that didn't help me the previous twelve months when I struggled to pay my cell phone bill or wasted time fending off threats of disconnection due to nonpayment. Reviewing your receipts and bill statements for accuracy is one of the surest ways to combat this problem.

## Communicate with Lenders

As a newly single mother with more day-to-day demands, I could not afford to work a second job or consistent overtime hours. I needed to find a way to eliminate or greatly reduce many of my essential expenses. My housing costs ate away at a huge chunk of my monthly income even after saving a few hundred dollars by cutting several expenses. One of the most important things I've learned is the power of communication.

Communicating with my lenders and letting them know that I was experiencing financial hardship helped me save thousands of dollars within a few minutes of being on the phone. You would be amazed at how much your providers are willing to assist you when you communicate with them. I ignored collection calls at first, because I wasn't ready to face the music of my own financial situation, and I was definitely not ready to admit it out loud to someone I owed money to.

Most collection companies are trained to pay attention to "hot words" when working with a client. They are actively listening for you to mention words like "hardship" or "change of income or employment" and, in my case, "divorce," before offering hardship programs to assist you if you don't know how to ask for them yourself.

## Lower Your Expenses

I took an entire day to search every service and provider I owed money to and gathered their contact information so that I could begin making calls. Working in collections can be a very stressful job, and by noon, the call volume goes up tremendously. Many working people can call only during their lunch break to inquire about their debts. Having an inside peek at collection agencies and call centers helped me prepare to spend the day on the phone asking for help.

I started with a very generic script that went something like this:

"Hey _____! My name is Dasha Kennedy, account number _____. I've been a loyal customer with you since _____. I want to continue my services with you, but I've fallen on hard times, and my financial circumstances have changed drastically. What hardship or discount programs do you have available that can help lower or pause my monthly payment?" In just a few sentences I was able to state who I was, provide my account information, describe my problem, and ask for solutions.

Although I was nervous on those first few calls, they resulted in being admitted to several default programs and getting fees waived, payments lowered, and balances eliminated. I realized that communication is the best form of currency when trying to reduce debt.

Here are some other scripts you can use when contacting your lenders:

**Paying the bill in full:** "Hi, I'm calling about my bill. I see that the balance is $_____, but I can pay $_____ today and settle the bill with a $0 balance."

**Cell phone bill script:** "Hi, I was looking at my plan, and it's getting pretty expensive. Could you tell me what other plans you have that would save me money?"

**Credit card interest script:** "Hello, I'm _____. I have a _____ card and have been a loyal customer with you since _____. Recently, I've been looking into other credit cards that provide a better value with a lower interest rate. I prefer to stick with my current card, but there are some good offers out there. Given my payment and credit history, can you help me lower my APR on this card today?"

**General bill script:** "Hello, my name is _____ and I've been a customer since_____. I'd like to keep my service with you, but my monthly bill is becoming expensive. I've seen that other companies offer similar plans at lower rates. Are there any discounts or promotions you can offer to help lower my bill?"

The goal is to help you work smarter, not harder, by finding ways to reduce your spending and allocate the money you already have toward debt elimination instead.

## Write It Down

For my debt elimination journey to become embedded in my brain, I put it in writing. Instead of using spreadsheets and apps to track my progress or manage my debt payments, I went old-school. I grabbed a pencil and paper and made a list of all my debt payments, the minimum payment I could afford each month, the details of the hardship plan attached to each debt, and the estimated payoff date.

Why was writing out my debt important? Money management is psychological. I had to process my debt payments once with my own handwriting and again with my own eyes. Seeing your debt information in your own handwriting is a different type of accountability. There was no strategy for how to write them down—I didn't list my debts from smallest to largest—but I needed to get those numbers out of my head, off the collection letter notices, and onto a blank piece of paper.

That blank piece of paper acted as a symbol for a clean slate—the beginning of a journey that would help me change the way I view money forever.

## Choose a Debt Elimination Plan

There are two frequently recommended debt elimination plans:

- One plan starts with paying off the debt with the highest interest rate (the avalanche method).
- The other plan starts with paying off the debt that has the smallest balance (the snowball method).

I'm going to be honest with you: I'm always going to do the thing that'll cost me as little as possible each month. Yes, it may cost me more money in the long run, but completely cutting fun and excitement out of my life each month for the sake of paying down debt faster wasn't a realistic option.

Mathematically, if you sit down and count your debt dollar by dollar, the avalanche method seems like the best option, but what's best isn't what's easiest or most realistic in your specific circumstances. So I went with the plan that cost me the least amount of money each month and solely focused on eliminating debts with the smallest balance, the snowball method. I remember feeling excited to see my debt balances decrease little by little each month. Focusing on the smaller debt helped me build momentum and prevented me from taking on more debt payments than I could handle.

### Don't Bite Off More than You Can Chew

Think of your total debt balance like a cake. How would you eat a double-layer triple-chocolate cake? One slice and one bite at a time. It's the same way when it comes to eliminating debt. When I looked at the amount of debt I owed as one large number, it ate away at me as something I would never be able to pay off. I had already given up on the idea that I would be able to pay it off in a short amount of time, so I started to nibble away at my outstanding debt little by little, bite by bite.

The truth is that you'll save more money in the long run by paying off debt as soon as possible, but our brains don't always work that way because large numbers in such a short amount of time are intimidating. So, instead of paying off $20,000 in a short period, I calculated how many times I could break that $20,000 down over a longer period while still actively covering all my other financial obligations. Twenty thousand dollars over a period of 104 weeks (two years) is $192. Of course, $192 is easier to come up with than $20,000.

## Debt Elimination Challenge

In November 2021, I started to see a ton of news articles discussing the fact that most millennials would go into 2022 with additional debt because of holiday spending. More than a third of Americans go into debt for the holidays and add over a grand to what they already owe.[3] About a quarter of us still have debt from the previous holiday season.[4] This season can get expensive fast, especially for families, because we believe (and advertisers outright tell us) that spending a ridiculous amount of money on our children, family, and friends is directly connected to joy. Who wouldn't want to see their children happy?

---

3   https://www.lendingtree.com/credit-cards/study/average-holiday-debt/#:~:text=Most%20 notably%2C%20those%20who%20took,at%20an%20average%20of%20%241%2C100.

4   https://wallethub.com/blog/holiday-shopping-survey/53828.

Between gifts, travel expenses, food, and decorations, those expenses can easily send us into the new year with over $1,000 more in debt. I often spent a lot of money over the holidays, especially after my divorce, when I was trying to maintain some normalcy, and then struggled with my mounting debt afterward. So I decided to create a community challenge to help keep others from adding to their financial burdens as we entered a new year.

My 45-Day Debt Elimination Challenge helped more than four hundred women collectively eliminate over $1 million in debt. The goal of this challenge was to aggressively attack one outstanding debt using actionable tactics instead of adding on new debt during the holiday season. For forty-five days straight, I provided the participants with an actionable financial challenge to complete by the end of each day. I consider "actionable" financial advice to be strategies and practices that can be accomplished easily and immediately. I used to consume hours of financial content each day and was usually left feeling confused and uncertain about where to start. Most of the financial content available didn't offer immediate action items and, in return, did not ease any of my financial burdens. I needed tactics I could implement and see results within the same day. **If you try out the 45-Day Debt Elimination Challenge yourself, I'd love to hear from you about the impact it had on your financial life.**[5]

A few of the challenges included organizing your debt, creating a budget, and knowing how the Fair Debt Collection Practices Act can protect you from predatory practices and harassment. I wanted to instill confidence in everyone in case they'd have to deal with threatening calls like the one I received. Another early challenge encouraged participants to communicate with their lenders and discuss payment arrangements for any outstanding debt. I created multiple scripts for

---

5    https://tbbgdigital.com/products/momentum-over-math-45-day-debt-elimination-
     challenge.

the participants to prepare for the calls, like those I shared above. I hope you try them out for yourself and let me know if you were able to reduce or eliminate a debt. Using my script, one participant reported that she got a debt of more than $11,000 eliminated by simply calling and communicating with her provider.

Another challenge focused on getting familiar with what's coming in and out of your bank account. This was the toughest but also most beneficial challenge. I asked each participant to pull their bank statements or transaction history from the last ninety days, highlight every nonessential purchase, and calculate the amount spent. In the middle of the night, I received an email from one woman telling me she had completed the challenge and was in disbelief that she had spent $17,000 on nonessentials. She was determined to make a change now that she recognized some of her habits.

In addition to the big-picture strategies and time-intensive challenges, I shared a few of my favorite tricks to make paying off debt easier and quicker:

- Switching to cash only to reduce spending
- Deleting your credit card information from online checkouts
- Canceling all unused subscriptions
- Unsubscribing from email newsletters and brand advertising that tempt you to spend money
- Instituting "no spend" days where you cover only necessities
- Unfollowing social media accounts that give you FOMO

The participants in the Debt Elimination Challenge shared their progress in a private Facebook group to hold each other accountable for their goals. You can do this with a friend, sibling, or spouse who's also interested in eliminating debt so you can support each other and offer accountability outside structured programs or groups. This built-in accountability, paired with truly actionable advice and turning an overwhelming process into manageable steps, helped people get started quickly and get some instant relief. These early small wins got people motivated to keep going, chipping away at their debt consistently. Sure, being able to pay off debt in a short period of time is impressive, but whom are we trying to impress? I don't want my journey to eliminate debt to be impressive—I want it to be effective.

## My Final Debt Payment

It took me five years to pay off the $20,000 worth of debt while recovering from my divorce and adjusting to my new life as a single mom. Debt can take over your life, especially when you don't see the light at the end of the tunnel. My debt was not just a financial strain but also a constant reminder of one of the most gut-wrenching experiences of my life. Chipping away at my debt little by little helped me build momentum that was accompanied by psychological benefits I never expected. I felt a new sense of competence, hope, and freedom.

When I made my final debt payment, I cried with relief, not just because I no longer had to carry the financial burden, but also because I finally felt some closure about the painful divorce that led to accumulating all that debt in the first place.

## Debt Elimination Checklist

### 1. IDENTIFY YOUR DEBT

Who is your creditor, and how much do you owe them? What's your interest percentage, minimum monthly payment, and due date?

### 2. REVIEW YOUR CREDIT REPORT

Follow the instructions in chapter 8 about how to access your annual free credit report.

### 3. OPEN ALL YOUR MAIL

Now is the perfect time to start going through all your mail, organizing it, and writing down all the contact information from the current creditor.

### 4. MONITOR BILL STATEMENTS FOR ACCURACY

You can't fix what you can't see. Opening your mail and facing the bills and collection notices head-on is the first step in monitoring your statements for inaccuracies.

### 5. COMMUNICATING WITH LENDERS

Most collection companies are actively listening for you to mention words like "hardship" or "change of income or employment" before offering hardship programs to assist you, but you can also directly ask for them.

### 6. LOWER YOUR EXPENSES

Use the call scripts I've shared to call your creditors and see if you can get admitted to default programs, get fees waived, have payments lowered, or eliminate balances.

### 7. WRITE IT DOWN

Money management is psychological. I needed to get those numbers out of my head, off the collection letter notices, and onto a blank piece of paper. Seeing your debt information in your own handwriting is a different type of accountability.

### 8. CHOOSE A DEBT ELIMINATION PLAN

Start paying off the debt with the highest interest rate (the avalanche method) or the debt that has the smallest balance (the snowball method). I used the snowball method, which helped me build momentum and prevented me from taking on more debt payments than I could handle.

## 9. DON'T BITE OFF MORE THAN YOU CAN CHEW

Pay off debt in small increments to gain confidence and an emotional boost while maintaining a financial cushion, reasonable quality of life, and the consistent momentum you need to keep going until you've eliminated your debt.

# CHAPTER 10

# Love Don't Cost a Thing (Marriage and Divorce)

When I stood at the front of the small church filled with a few dozen of my closest friends, I entered one of the most complex financial contracts of a woman's life—marriage. I was only twenty-five at the time and had never had a substantive conversation about money with the man I was about to marry. We entered marriage as a couple on paper but as individuals when it came to money. I had no clue that although we earned, spent, saved, and invested our own money, all our individual choices would impact each other and our family. Neither one of us knew what we were doing when it came to finances, and I felt awkward about having difficult conversations about these complicated topics. Avoiding those discussions felt easier than dealing with any potential conflicts.

For a while, everything mostly fell into place as we both paid bills, took care of the kids, and made sure we didn't go hungry or sat in the dark with the lights shut off. But there was no plan, no designated responsibilities, no shared values. And that would eventually become our downfall.

## Smart About Money ≠ Cynical About Love

I'm not anti-marriage, anti-love, or a cynical man-hater, but I believe women need to hope for the best while also building safeguards, just like taking out life insurance, car insurance, or building an emergency fund. One of the biggest financial risks a woman takes in her life is getting married, because it often leads to a disruption in your individual financial life like putting your education or career on hold while taking on essential but unpaid caregiving labor, which can result in decreased income, loss of retirement contributions, and reduced savings and investments.

Money problems are one of the primary issues in romantic relationships, whether you're married or not. My advice to women, and to my younger self, is countercultural to what is expected of women and the opposite of what's shown in the media: **"It's not necessary for me to prove my commitment to a relationship by compromising my financial security."**

Every time someone asks me when they should start talking about money to their dates, significant others, partners, or spouses, I say as soon as possible. It doesn't have to be heavy or serious from the beginning, but why not start on your first date?

- Who will pay the bill?
- Will you alternate or split the check?
- If one of you feels responsible or reluctant to pick up the tab, why is that?

Yes, it can be awkward, but it's better than getting stuck in a relationship where your partner's money decisions affect you negatively, but now you own a car or house together, are on the same lease, or are responsible for taking care of your children. I wish I'd pushed through the awkwardness of not knowing what to discuss and where to start with my ex-husband, before our noncommunication caused serious problems.

As you get to know someone, you can learn a lot about their money mindset from discussing regular dating topics such as their family background, cultural upbringing, hobbies, and activities.

- Do they drop concepts or principles they've learned from their grandparents, at their church, or in school?
- Do they have a steady job, talk about investing, or "forget" their wallet a lot?
- Do they have career ambitions or float from job to job?
- Do they espouse outdated beliefs about family and marriage?

You can listen first for those clues and ask follow-up questions to learn more. In the early stages, listening and curiosity will give you a general sense before you move to direct money conversations as your connection progresses.

### Are You Willing to Have Uncomfortable Money Conversations?

Forget about the early fights about how much to spend on your wedding or honeymoon. That's just the beginning! How do you feel about life insurance, retirement savings, and emergency funds? Financial compatibility is key in dating and marriage and should not be a taboo topic. Financial compatibility doesn't mean you both need to make the same amount of money, but you should understand each other's financial behaviors and values. Having these conversations is uncomfortable, but not nearly as painful as learning you don't share the same values when it matters for your financial survival.

At the end of 2013, a few months into our marriage, I came home to an empty house after work. My then-husband and I had gotten into a big argument, and he'd left while I was gone. The stress and emotional toll of the fight were weighing on my mind, but as it turned out, this would not be my biggest problem. When I went to pay our rent that night, I was shocked to find his half gone. While we didn't always split the rent consistently, he had sporadically contributed to rent and bills, and I would often make plans with my extra funds, whether it was for groceries, bus fare, or cab rides. But on that day, I was completely blindsided to find that his half had been taken back when he left.

I didn't have the funds to make up for his missing half, so I was sent straight back to the predatory payday lending cycle to cover his portion. It was gut-wrenching to realize that I was vulnerable to such financial instability, even in my marriage. I chose this person, but my kids didn't. I remember feeling low, guilty, embarrassed, and even pathetic that I had put my livelihood, as well as my children's livelihoods, into the hands of someone else. I made the decision this would never happen to me again. I would have a backup plan for my backup plan.

Although this was the beginning of the end, he moved back in a few weeks later. It sucks to say that this horrible incident wasn't the catalyst that made me realize the marriage was too far gone. I still needed his help with the kids, who were only two and six at the time. Our financial lives were intertwined, although we never had any money discussions before we got married. I was stuck, at least for a while.

Shortly after the blowup fight, I got a better job with better pay and benefits. I wanted to use this career opportunity as a jumping-off point to make long-term financial planning a priority. One of the first things on my list was getting life insurance, so I set up a meeting with an agent to come to our house and discuss different policy terms with us. I let my husband know about the appointment and how important this conversation was to me.

I remember feeling embarrassed when he got up in the middle of our discussion because he wanted to go play basketball instead. My mouth literally dropped. There were plenty of red flags before this moment, but nothing gave me clarity like seeing this unmistakable proof of our misaligned financial priorities and values. That one incident was the last in a long line, illuminating our fundamental lack of communication and partnership in financial matters. It was enlightening and heartbreaking.

If I'd had the life insurance conversation with my ex-husband before we got married, I might have realized sooner that we had different perspectives on our financial responsibilities. Looking back, I now see that he seemed comfortable with me shouldering most of the responsibility for our family's long-term financial security, while he wasn't as equally invested. I might have realized earlier that this would be a significant barrier to building a stable and secure future together.

### Cultural, Familial, and Personal Beliefs About Partnership

While conversations about practical matters such as life insurance, retirement, savings, or student loans are incredibly important, so is questioning our historical, cultural, and familial beliefs about partnership and marriage. Historically, women were considered their fathers' property, and marriage was necessary for a woman's physical and economic survival. This is why fathers "give away" their daughters on their wedding day. It's property changing hands. It wasn't until the 1800s that states started passing laws allowing women to own property and gain some control over their wages and estates. Often these conversations help us consciously evaluate our beliefs and question the ones that are outdated and have no place in modern relationships. We've certainly made progress as a society, but many harmful ideas surrounding value contributions in marriage linger.

### Adding Kids to the Mix

Do you agree on if, when, and how many kids you want? Will you take care of or provide for kids differently if you bring them into the marriage, rather than have them with your current partner? Do you feel financially responsible for each other's kids from previous relationships? If you decide to have children, who will stay home with them, and for how long? How will you split parenting duties and support each other's careers?

If you agree on one of you taking on most of the childcare responsibilities, including staying out of the workforce for a certain period of time, you'll need to have conversations about how this impacts both your savings and retirement contributions. Since women often take on this responsibility without compensation or a plan on how the partnership is accountable for creating financial stability for everyone, this can result in an unstable retirement.

### Individual, Couple, and Family Responsibilities

What contributions are expected of each household member? Will children get an allowance for chores? Will everyone in the family save together for joint activities, entertainment, or trips, or is this the sole responsibility of the parents?

You can have weekly, monthly, and yearly review and goal-setting conversations for personal, couple, and family financial matters. You should also trust but verify, meaning periodically review and verify all joint financial accounts and investments. You may think this is paranoid, but when I still worked at the bank, I spoke to many sobbing women after a divorce or the death of their spouse who were completely unaware that their home was in foreclosure or their name wasn't on the financial accounts, contrary to their partner's statements.

### Agreeing on a Budget

Your joint budget will help you deal with discrepancies in pay. More than likely, one spouse will make more money, and it's important to remember that 50/50 is fair but not always equitable. Instead of paying half of everything, you can also consider paying a specific percentage of your income to the household account and keeping the rest for yourself. This discussion should also include personal and shared debt and how you each prioritize paying them off.

## Maintaining Joint and Separate Accounts

How will you structure household budgets and accounts to manage family expenses and savings while maintaining individual access to personal checking and savings accounts? I'm not against joint accounts for household expenses, but I highly recommend you have your own checking and savings accounts, as well as credit cards that are only in your name. Just because something is in your name only doesn't mean you're hiding anything from your partner. It can be a joint value that each of you maintains financial independence. You're still an individual, not half a couple, and therefore have your own life and experience outside your relationship.

## Making Decisions Together

Take responsibility for educating yourself on matters of budgeting, saving, investments, and debt management as well as understanding your own and your partner's needs, wants, hang-ups, challenges, and goals. Your individual knowledge will help you advocate for your personal, couple, and family goals so you can be an equal partner in financial decision-making. This goes for your partner too. Do you want to be with someone who has no clue what it's like to be a woman in this country with all the related financial implications and, therefore, can't take that into consideration when you make decisions together? I made that mistake once, but it won't happen again.

I'll never get tired of talking about individual financial literacy, access, and empowerment, especially for married women. You can believe in love, deeply trust your partner, and still keep your own money. You can build wealth individually and together by assessing financial compatibility, discussing expectations, maintaining financial independence, and focusing on collaboration and transparency in your partnership or marriage.

## Signing a Prenup

A prenuptial agreement (prenup) is a contract you sign before you get married that lays out how finances will be handled during your marriage and in the event of a divorce.

I'm so tired of the tropes surrounding gender and prenups. If a man wants a prenup to protect the wealth he built on his own before the marriage, and the woman doesn't want to sign it, she's obviously (insert eye roll here) a gold digger. But if a woman wants a prenup to do the same, it means she doesn't love the man, and the marriage is doomed from the start.

So, if you wonder whether it's dumb to go into marriage planning for a divorce, consider if it's as dumb as having to comply with whatever marital laws are already in place in your state. Even if you don't believe in prenups, you will abide by one—your own or the one the state created for you.

## What Goes into a Prenup?

The specifics of what you'll want to include are based on your individual circumstances, local laws, and personal preferences, but there are several key considerations:

- **Asset and Debt Division:** How will you divide, pay off, or liquidate any real estate, investments, businesses, or vehicles that you have acquired before and during the marriage? How will you pay off joint debt?
- **Spousal Support:** Alimony terms including amount, duration, and conditions to modify or terminate the support.
- **Inheritance and Estate Plans:** Who will inherit what, especially important if state law needs to be waived or modified.
- **Retirement Benefits:** What happens to pensions, 401(k) plans, and IRAs? Contributions you make during your marriage— even to individual accounts—become joint assets.
- **Joint Expenses and Bank Accounts:** How will household expenses, savings, and joint accounts be managed?

- **Provisions for Children from Previous Relationships:** How will inheritance rights and financial interests be managed?
- **Conflict Resolution:** How will you resolve disputes about the prenup terms, including mediation or arbitration?
- **Sunset Clause:** Will this agreement expire after a certain period of marriage if both parties agree?

When you talk through the specifics you want to include in your prenup, that's another chance to double-check if you're both on the same page. Movies, music, TV, and loudmouths on social media still espouse some version of "women take half of the money they didn't earn during a divorce." While it's true that we're all constantly learning and growing, do you really want to spend all your time and energy explaining to a partner why this couldn't be further from the truth? How much bandwidth do you have to educate a grown adult on the basics of invisible and unpaid labor and how that impacts men and women differently in marriage and divorce? There is an opportunity to educate, but it's not *your* job.

If women globally received minimum wage for their unpaid labor (child and elder care, cleaning, cooking, family management, etc.), it would have added $10.9 trillion to the global economy in one year.[1] If we're talking only about women in the US, the total would have been $1.5 trillion. These massive numbers are hard to process, so let's break them down further. Over the course of an average eight-year marriage,[2] that would be $92,656 worth of unpaid labor for one woman. So, women miss out on nearly six figures during their marriages and still have to deal with the cultural stereotype of being gold diggers.

This type of thinking can be just plain ignorance or a sign of financial abuse. Either way, you have a right and an obligation to protect

---

1    https://www.nytimes.com/interactive/2020/03/04/opinion/women-unpaid-labor.html.

2    https://www.census.gov/content/dam/Census/library/publications/2021/demo/p70-167.pdf.

yourself, including signing an ironclad prenup or getting the hell out of that relationship before it's too late. All the money conversations, including regarding prenups, can help you spot red flags that hint at unhealthy financial dynamics or even abuse.

## Financial Abuse Red Flags— When Money Becomes a Weapon

Money should empower, not overpower. Money has the potential to provide us with a sense of security, stability, and freedom. However, when it's used as a weapon to control, manipulate, or intimidate others, it becomes a tool of abuse. It's time we take this taboo topic out of the shadows and educate everyone on the red flags pointing to potential financial abuse:

- A spouse who controls all the finances and doesn't allow the other person to spend any money without permission.
- A parent who threatens to cut off financial support unless their child does what they want.
- An employer who retaliates against staff for speaking up about workplace issues by cutting hours or manufacturing frivolous write-ups.
- A friend who constantly asks to borrow money and becomes angry or hostile when the other person says no.
- A government agency or institution that unfairly denies or revokes financial assistance for benefits to individuals or groups.
- A financial adviser who recommends products not solely in their client's best interest but to earn a commission.
- A family member who takes control of an elderly relative's finances without their consent.

As a society, we're making slow progress in having conversations about physical, sexual, verbal, and emotional abuse, but we rarely talk about financial abuse. So many of us are uncomfortable talking about finances that financial abuse seems almost invisible, silent, and hidden from view.

Financial abuse is a valid reason to initiate divorce, but of course it's also a major barrier to separate from a spouse who holds all the financial power in the relationship. There are several reputable websites and resources to support you on this path, such as Surviving Economic Abuse[3] and the National Network to End Domestic Violence.[4]

## The *D* Word

My divorce marked a dramatic and sudden change in my financial responsibilities after sharing the burden of household expenses, even as chaotic as that arrangement was. Once we separated and I became 100 percent responsible for the household expenses on only one income, I realized how vulnerable I had made myself. Even though I now had a better job, I immediately knew that my growth opportunities would be limited because being responsible for everything would make it impossible to work on additional projects or pick up overtime. I knew I'd have to stay financially afloat while learning a new role and continue taking care of my children and household, all while going through a divorce. My time, energy, and emotional and mental capacity would be strained as much as my finances.

Divorce is common, but that doesn't make it any less financially and emotionally draining. Women over fifty experience a 45 percent decrease in standard of living after divorce, and household income drops 23–40 percent among all divorced women.[5] About one in five women fall into poverty postdivorce, one in four lose health insurance, and one in three lose their homes. Add to that that three in four moms

---

3   https://survivingeconomicabuse.org/i-need-help/.

4   https://nnedv.org/spotlight_on/financial-abuse-empowerment/.

5   https://www.ncbi.nlm.nih.gov/pmc/articles/PMC8599059/.

with child support orders don't receive their full payment, and you have the perfect financial storm.[6] Financial security is one of the most significant considerations women factor in when deciding whether to stay in an unhappy marriage or get divorced. Especially when kids are involved. Being fully aware of your financial situation isn't an option—it's necessary.

## You're 100 Percent Financially Responsible Overnight—Now What?

The reality of household income and expenses being split—however unequal—one day and then being solely responsible for all the bills the very next day was a huge wake-up call. No longer sharing financial responsibilities was tangible evidence of the end of our marriage and a daily reminder. All of a sudden, I was at the mercy of someone else's emotions, which made me even more financially vulnerable while entirely responsible for all household expenses covering rent, utilities, childcare, food, and transportation. It's important to not let fear and grief paralyze you, but spring into action as soon as you can.

### Get an Accurate Financial Picture

If you haven't been on top of your finances, this will be harder but not impossible. Collect all financial documents (paper or digital), including bank statements, tax returns, pay stubs, mortgage records, car loans, credit card statements, etc. This will help you understand your collective assets and liabilities and give you a clear picture of your financial situation. This also includes educating yourself on state laws regarding marriage and divorce. You need to have accurate information so that you can position yourself for fair negotiations.

I didn't have savings, an emergency fund, or even a plan for managing day-to-day household expenses without my husband's

---

6   https://yourdivorcequestions.org/how-will-divorce-affect-me-financially/.

income. Money is incredibly emotional, and divorce amplifies that, but rushing to finalize a divorce because you just want to get it over with is one of many reasons why so many women experience real financial damage. It's important to get a complete accounting of all that's worth fighting for to maintain as much financial security as possible.

### Open Your Own Accounts Immediately

If you don't have your own bank account yet, open one immediately. There's no judgment if you've never built financial independence or let it go by the wayside during your marriage. No need to beat yourself up about it, but you do need to make some moves right away. The first step to start building financial independence from your spouse is getting your own account. Divorce is usually not a quick process, so you need a safe place to deposit your money or start your savings for months or years to come while you're navigating divorce proceedings and waiting until your financial lives have been legally separated.

### Create Your Divorce Budget

Also known as the "when everything goes to shit" budget. You can refer to chapter 1, where I explain all four types of budgets I recommend setting up. This emergency budget drastically reduces your living expenses to the bare minimum, giving you a chance to get through your separation or divorce without compromising your basic needs. This essentials-only budget covers food, housing, utilities, medication, transportation, basic clothing and hygiene items, childcare, and insurance. Your essentials will be slightly different, but make sure you include only your absolute bare necessities.

### Update All Your Documents

If you've created a will or estate, update beneficiaries immediately. The same goes for any life insurance policies or any other assets, savings accounts, retirement savings, or stocks that may not be included in your estate planning or in case you don't have a comprehensive will set up yet.

## Build a Separate Credit History

Creditors do not care about your divorce or what the court says. If your name is on an account, card, loan, or mortgage, creditors will consider you liable, no matter what. You can be sued for the debt. If the court has ordered your ex to pay a certain debt and he doesn't, you can sue him for not honoring the divorce decree, but the downside is that you'll have to go back to court. This can turn into an expensive and lengthy process that will not keep the creditors from coming after you.

We already discussed the importance of building good credit, but during divorce proceedings this is even more important. Whether you haven't started yet or want to protect your good credit score, you need to pay attention to this because it will affect your ability to access housing, emergency credit lines, and job prospects. If possible, apply for a credit card in your own name. If you have joint cards from your marriage, you are responsible for the debt. It doesn't matter if you never used the card and your spouse charged thousands of dollars. If both of your names are on the card, both of you are considered equally responsible. Joint cards equal joint debt. The responsibility for the purchases made postseparation varies state by state. That's why it's essential to learn the marital laws in your state so you know what you're dealing with.

## Get All the Help You Can

If you have family members or friends who've gone through a divorce before, they not only can offer emotional support, but likely have practical experience in navigating your state's family law and may share with you what mistakes to avoid or which resources to access immediately. Whether you have questions about child support, alimony, or splitting assets and paying off debt, your family and friends can't give you legal advice, but they can share their experiences. This can be helpful in doing your own research and creating a list of questions for accessing legal help.

### Yes, You Do Need Legal Help

The first question is often, well, how am I supposed to afford a lawyer? Maybe your income was already low before, and a separation or divorce is only adding to your financial stress, so why would you even try to get legal help? Family law is confusing, and even if you do have a prenup, there will be important aspects, such as child custody and child support, that must be agreed on by both parties or decided by the court. With everything else you'll need to deal with, such as figuring out childcare and housing, you do need professional help to ensure you're not being taken advantage of legally.

If you can't afford a lawyer, there are services and programs available to help, including:

**The American Bar Association, abafreelegalanswers.org:** This virtual legal clinic offers advice from pro bono attorneys in your state. You go to the website, answer a few questions to determine your eligibility, and then ask your question. A lawyer will respond for free if your question concerns a civil matter, which includes divorce and custody, but not criminal matters, such as assault, drug abuse, or child endangerment.

**Legal Aid, lawhelp.org:** This nonprofit agency offers free legal help to low-income people. If you don't meet the income eligibility, you can still get self-help resources. The great thing about legal aid is that they somewhat specialize in issues affecting low-income families, including housing and public benefits, in addition to being experts at dealing with family law and domestic violence. This means you can get help for many of the other issues that often come with divorce, such as financial instability impacting your housing or childcare, or navigating public benefits.

If you're a military veteran, you can access free legal help through Stateside Legal (statesidelegal.org) or find resources specific to your state by going to the National Center for State Courts (ncsc.org). Many states have at least basic resources or self-help law centers. Finally, if you have a law school in your city or state, it may offer free legal clinics or advice from law students supervised by professors.

## How to Enforce Your Prenup

If you have a prenup, good for you! If you both agree to follow the prenup, great. If not, your lawyer can communicate with your spouse's lawyer, or you can file an action with the court. Remember, prenups can't include child custody or child support stipulations, so you'll have to work this out separately.

## Consider Mediation over Court

What's worse is that we often forget that there's a period between splitting up and officially divorcing or getting a legal financial agreement in place. This means assets might be tied up in litigation while you lose the second income, but you don't get any child support and still have to make payments on any debt accumulated in the marriage. That's the real danger zone of financial vulnerability.

I wish I'd at least tried mediation, instead of experiencing a sixteen-month legal battle, during which I wasn't just emotionally exhausted, but experienced courtroom and workplace bias. The judge, at one point, decided to extend our hearing for two weeks just to allow my ex to show up. After I'd presented at all the hearings (taking the bus, of course) and lost wages for each day I had to appear in court, the judge cut my ex some extra slack. I tried to explain to the judge that I was the sole financial provider for my kids and that I lost income every time my lawyer and I showed up to a hearing that my ex missed. Extending the hearing would cause problems at work, and I would lose more pay. The judge didn't listen. My ex still didn't show up. I lost more wages. And on top of that, my manager at work made this process a living hell. I had to speak with her privately in the stairway, crying because she denied my request for time off and having to involuntarily tell her about my divorce to humanize my requests and get them approved.

Within a few short months, I'd gone from a top-tier employee to being seen as less focused, less committed, and unreliable. Not because I woke up and decided to be a bad employee, but because I decided to get a divorce, which required my presence and attention outside the office while caring for my kids and dealing with my no-show ex and an indifferent judge.

Instead of leaving it up to a family court judge, you can try mediation as an "alternative dispute resolution process that involves a neutral third party (a mediator)."[7] Some states or family courts may ask you to do mediation before going to court, in an attempt to help ex-spouses to mutually agree on childcare and support, living arrangements, or medical expenses. The pros of mediation are that it's often cheaper and faster than going to court and that you have more control over the final agreement, rather than letting a judge decide. The cons are potentially having to go back and forth and wasting time on discussions with an unwilling or hostile ex-spouse.

You can find a mediator in your state by using the Academy of Professional Mediators' directory[8] or getting in touch with your local family court.

## Divorce Is an Evolution, Not a Dissolution

It's possible to reframe the financial impact of divorce as an evolution rather than a dissolution. If you've been following my journey from the beginning, you've seen firsthand how my divorce unraveled my

---

7   https://www.findlaw.com/family/child-custody/child-custody-mediation-faq.html.

8   https://apfmnet.org/find-a-mediator/.

entire life—especially my finances. But somehow, I found the power of perseverance I didn't know I had. I rebuilt my life from scratch, rediscovering my financial identity as a divorced woman. It wasn't easy, but it taught me resilience and self-reliance, two essential qualities necessary to overcome the financial impact of divorce.

The financial and emotional toll of the divorce was profound in every aspect of my life, even though we didn't own a house together and I'd just gotten a better-paying job. In other words, I didn't have it as bad as it could have been, and it was still one of the most financially and emotionally draining situations of my entire life. This is to say, it's going to be hard, no matter what. And yet I don't regret my decision and still consider it an act of radical self-love.

I'm in awe of every woman who makes that choice, knowing full well how hard it's going to be. If you're in the process of making this decision, I hope my experience and recommendations will make your situation feel less overwhelming. You will come out the other side stronger.

## Divorce Checklist—Do This Right Now!

1.  Educate yourself on state laws regarding marriage and divorce.

2.  Get a lawyer. If you can't afford a lawyer, visit your state's court website to learn about any self-help services available locally, including legal aid programs, pro bono lawyers, and law clinics or workshops at your local law school.

3.  Collect all financial documents (paper or digital), including bank statements, tax returns, pay stubs, mortgage records, car loans, credit card statements, etc.

4.  Open a separate bank account if you don't already have one and

update all your financial documents, such as wills, estates, and life insurance policies.

5. Switch to your emergency budget immediately or create one if you haven't already. Refer to chapter 1 for instructions on how to do this.

6. Reach out to family and friends for help, identify community, state, and federal resources, and get all the support you qualify for.

7. Try mediation instead of going to court for a potentially cheaper and faster resolution.

8. Enforce your prenup if you have one.

9. Start building a separate credit history immediately if you haven't already done so.

10. Prioritize self-care as much as possible during the divorce process. This is a marathon, not a sprint, unfortunately, and you'll need to pace yourself and keep up your strength.

# CHAPTER 11

# Deal or No Deal (Negotiation)

I made a salary of $32,000 at a company that I'd been working at for five years. Our management changed several times during the first three years of my employment, sometimes leaving my team with no direct supervisor. It was there that I ended up in leadership roles without the title or pay. I organized team meetings, worked the overflow cases that my team members could not complete to avoid any negative feedback on our team, and stayed late to finish up tough cases that often resulted in me missing the bus.

And then I was asked to help test a new product. This product was designed to shift a process we'd been doing manually into an electronic form. The catch was that I *still* had to do the job manually, but now I also had to repeat the task electronically on the new system. In other words, I was doubling my work, doing everything that I had already been doing, but twice. I was also charged with running and managing this new system on my team. All this was expected to be done in the same already-jammed eight-hour workday and for the same pay. It was a lot, but I saw this as a positive development. The fact that I was viewed as responsible enough to take this on had to mean that my manager was noticing my good work and that a raise was on the horizon!

As I got this new system off the ground, I often worked beyond those eight hours and was rarely offered overtime. I was constantly overwhelmed and exhausted, to the point that I even cried on a few occasions. One Friday, I was wrapping up and preparing to leave when a senior colleague revealed to me that there were about eighteen incomplete cases in this new electronic system. I advised her that my day was ending and my regular workload, which was a priority, took my entire shift. My colleague, under pressure from the ongoing company-wide issues with the system, expressed how important it was for me to stay and resolve the cases. However, I was already anxious about catching my bus because missing it would have serious consequences. It meant I would be late to pick up my children from day care, incur a late fee I couldn't afford, and further disrupt my already-tight schedule and budget. Despite my concerns, when my colleague mentioned "we're going to get in trouble if this isn't handled," I felt compelled to stay. Tears started to run down my face while I put my purse down and got back in my seat to complete those tasks. But I still got the work done.

After a year of working like this, I was sure that the moment for recognition had arrived. I walked into my boss's office feeling excited. I sat down in the chair across from her and felt my heart jump as she pushed a piece of paper across the table. I flipped it over to see that she had circled the amount of my raise on it. The moment had finally arrived! I looked down in anticipation and saw that the raise was . . . seventeen cents an hour.

Now, I'm known for having what people call a "resting b-tch face," and I knew I could not hide what I was feeling on the inside. As I stared at that piece of paper, my excitement quickly changed into disbelief and then disappointment. Seventeen cents an hour? After all my hard work, dedication, and anticipation, this was the reward? I felt so many things—frustration, anger, and a clear sense of being undervalued. Was I foolish to somehow think my boss would pay me more than seventeen cents? Was I foolish to expect more? I couldn't help but feel let down by my boss, by the workforce, and even by myself for thinking a company would give me more simply because I worked harder. Foolish, right?

I'd love to tell you that I summoned up all my confidence and negotiated the salary I was worth . . . but I didn't. Instead, I held my tears back and stood up to leave the room. As I walked toward the door, my boss warned me, "Don't discuss this with your colleagues. Some people didn't get a raise at all." Was this a threat or some type of gentle reminder? It seemed like both. As I walked out of her office, a wave of self-doubt came over me. The voice in my head whispered, "You should be thankful for anything at all." It was hard not to compare my situation with others who might not have gotten anything, and that guilt only added an extra layer of disappointment.

This stands out as a particularly extreme moment when I knew I deserved more than I got at work, but it's certainly not the only time it happened. Like most women, I've been in the position of being overworked and underpaid many times. From the time I was sixteen years old until I was thirty, I believed this was a temporary situation. I believed that if I continued to work hard and go above and beyond, my efforts would be recognized and I would be rewarded with an increase in salary that would take all my financial worries away. I truly thought that's how things worked. I'm not the only one to feel this way. Research shows that many women of color feel "an instinct to stay silent and be grateful for what [we] have" due to a very "reasonable fear of backlash."[9] Black women especially experience that "revealing ambitious intentions and a healthy self-esteem caused [us]

---

9    https://hbr.org/2022/01/negotiating-as-a-woman-of-color.

to be misinterpreted as angry, difficult, or aggressive."[10] Women of color still deal with "standing out while also being marginalized [ . . . ] heightening expectations that [we] conform and don't draw further attention to [ourselves]."

Based on these beliefs, I was on a constant quest to prove myself—a quest that often meant I took on more work and stress than I could handle. Even after I'd been doing this for years and years and reached the point that I was generally burned-out from working so hard for so long yet still scrambling to pay my bills, I still believed this was temporary. Not once in fifteen years did I ever negotiate my pay, because I never felt confident or comfortable enough to do so. Also, not once did an employer ever recognize me for all my hard work in any sort of significant monetary way. It wasn't until I became an entrepreneur that I finally learned to stand up for my own worth and negotiate terms that felt equitable to me.

Unfortunately, I know I'm not alone in this. For decades, studies showed that women were not asking for more money in the workplace. It became a convenient way to blame women for the gender wage gap, as if all of us didn't already know there were deeply ingrained cultural reasons that we felt like we couldn't ask for more. We thought we'd get punished, and we were right. Newer studies show that women now negotiate their salaries more than men and *still* get paid less.[11] I wish I was surprised, but I'm not.

It's time for this to change.

## Inherited Beliefs About Negotiation

Although we often don't consciously realize it, many of our beliefs about worth—financial and otherwise—are inherited from our family,

---

10    Ibid.

11    https://vcresearch.berkeley.edu/news/new-research-shatters-outdated-pay-gap-myth-women-dont-negotiate.

culture, and society. These beliefs can be passed down from generation to generation, and because they're so ingrained in us, they're often difficult to notice, much less question. In other words, these beliefs that aren't even necessarily ours become our reality. This is important to recognize when it comes to negotiation.

I grew up in a family that didn't talk about money in general; for whatever reason, it was treated as an uncomfortable topic that was avoided whenever possible. Now that I'm an adult with some experience under my belt, I understand that not only is negotiation normal, but it's a necessary skill that should be cultivated. It's something that I absolutely should have been doing, especially in those moments when I was offered a new job, changing roles, taking on new responsibilities, or reaching new levels of achievement—and you should be too. Negotiation is a part of life. Not once did I hear that growing up, though, so it never occurred to me that this was a muscle that I should strengthen and flex.

Because I didn't think of negotiation as a skill, I instead attached a lot of emotion and judgment to it. I believed that asking for what I was worth was somehow disrespectful and feared that I would look greedy or ungrateful if I were to ask for more money. Instead, I believed that I should be thankful just to have my foot in the door. I worried that if I made too much of a fuss or asked for too much, my employer would decide it was simpler and cheaper just to get rid of me, and that instead of ending up with more, I would end up with less. That was daunting, particularly in the years when I was just scraping by. This led to what I can now see is an ironic situation, but I know many people can relate: the more I needed a salary increase, the less likely I was to go to the negotiating table and ask for it.

Your company hired you because they see value in you and what you can do for the business. I know it may not feel like that since these words often go unspoken, so I hope that you will remind yourself of this fact in moments when you may feel unworthy of asking for more:

*if you have a job, you are worth the money.* Remember that this is the business world, and even though your company sees your value, they're still going to try to get you for an economical price. That's how business works.

Now let's take a moment to pause and reflect. What is the first thought that comes to your mind when you think about negotiating for a higher salary or expressing your worth in the workplace? Are there any beliefs that you hold about getting paid what you deserve or what is acceptable to ask for? What is the first thought or attitude that comes to mind?

Let's try this exercise:

- Write down three beliefs that you associate with negotiation and self-worth. Example: "If I ask for a raise, they'll decline and maybe just replace me instead."
- Review each belief you write down and ask yourself: Where did this belief come from? Is it from personal experience, a societal norm, or something that has been normalized in your family? Really challenge yourself to analyze the origin of those beliefs. Example: Your parents instilled in you that you should be grateful to have any job and not rock the boat, jeopardizing your security.
- Think about whether these beliefs serve you positively or hold you back. Have any of your beliefs on negotiation and self-worth helped you in the workforce? Can you reframe any of your negative beliefs into empowering beliefs? Example: "I have options. If I ask for a raise and my boss declines it, I can back up my request with evidence, I can negotiate other benefits or perks instead, or I can find a different position at a new company."
- Write down one positive affirmation or practice that you can adopt when it comes to expressing your worth in the workforce. Example: "Asking for a raise is an opportunity for me to

advocate for myself and an opportunity for my boss to show their appreciation for what I contribute to the company."

## Corporate Reality Check

It's up to you to reevaluate your beliefs, understanding of your own worth, and willingness to advocate for yourself through negotiation, because the reality is that no one else will, no matter how hard you work or how much you *should* be noticed. At the end of the day, business is driven by two things: results and a profitable bottom line. They're paying attention to whether objectives are being met, not how underpaid, overwhelmed, or burned-out you may be. Now, this doesn't mean that you can't positively impact both your salary and workload, but it does mean that you're responsible for advancing the discussions that will get you there, because business is not designed to be mindful of those things for you, no matter what the corporate culture might proclaim.

This begins way before you get to the point of work reviews or one-on-ones with your manager; it begins from the moment you're offered the job. Whether you think about it this way or not, agreeing to accept a position at a certain wage is a negotiation. It's important that you start to see it as such, because your company does, and that means they're starting with the lowest amount possible, with the expectation that you will negotiate to bring that starting salary higher. Although women negotiate as much as men now, we're still less likely to be successful in salary negotiations, and even if we are, we usually receive a smaller increase than men.[12] This is BS, but you should still ask, because otherwise the answer is already no.

The same idea applies to salary increases once you're in the door. Most of us were raised to believe that good work is noticed and rewarded, that your company will take some sort of ownership in this

---

12    https://doi.org/10.1111/irel.12214.

process. It would be nice if that were the case, and it would make *sense* if that were the case, because it's good business to keep loyal, productive employees happy, but it doesn't change the fact that it's usually not how things work in the corporate world. Beyond the standard cost-of-living increase, most employers expect that you will take charge of asking for increases. This means that if you abide by a set of beliefs that tell you that you shouldn't have these conversations, don't understand how negotiation works, or haven't honed the skill, chances are you're going to keep waiting around to be recognized.

There's one more corporate standard that it's important to know about when it comes to salary and negotiation—wage transparency. The vast majority of employers discourage employees from discussing salaries with colleagues, much like my boss did when I was awarded that seventeen-cent raise, although some employers convey this message less overtly than mine did. Still, I felt conflicted about keeping my seventeen-cent raise a secret. By that point, I'd worked with the same team for a few years, and keeping any information from them felt like a betrayal, like I was participating in a system where not everyone gets what they deserve. At the same time, I worried that if I did share the information, I'd face retaliation. No wonder most of us are worried to join a workers' union or engage in collective bargaining, even though most of us also believe that we deserve fair pay, safe working conditions, and a voice. This fear is valid. Technically, workers have the right to unionize, but companies often engage in barely legal "union busting" techniques, such as writing up or firing organizers for flimsy reasons, dragging out contract negotiations, and offering incentives and higher wages for nonunion employees or exclusively at nonunionized stores or locations.[13]

Still, unions have been vital in balancing the power dynamics between employers and employees through collective bargaining rather

---

13    https://www.fastcompany.com/91001266/the-worst-union-busters-of-2023.

than individual negotiations, achieving better pay and safer working conditions for entire industries. While the effectiveness of unions can vary between industries, I fully support workers' rights, and if I had the opportunity to unionize, I would take it.

It's clear to me now that the only party who benefits from silencing wage discussions among employees is *the company*. Let's take a moment to really sit with this phenomenon that most of us consider normal: Why on earth should what you make be a secret? Wouldn't it be helpful to discuss salaries with the people you're most comparable to, your coworkers? Shouldn't your earnings be close enough to a coworker of comparable experience and responsibilities that any information you learn from these conversations would only confirm your salary? The truth is that silence certainly doesn't help anyone in the workforce, and particularly women. This vacuum of information maintains pay disparities and inequities and keeps employees in the dark about their market value. It's through this silence that employees filling comparable roles can be paid different amounts for doing the same job. And by the way, silence also ensures that coworkers don't come together when negotiating pay, which is likely to be more effective than every (wo)man for herself. If we normalize being transparent about salaries and wages, things would start to shift in employees' favor. It would almost certainly create more fairness and equity in the workplace.

The lack of open discussion about wages is so prominent that many people believe doing so would somehow be in violation of "the rules." In reality, it's nothing more than a cultural norm. Under the National Labor Relations Act, most employees have the legal right to discuss their salaries,[14] even though it may feel culturally off-limits at your company. It's true that, in a worst-case scenario, some companies might even indirectly penalize you for having such discussions—though if

---

14   https://www.nlrb.gov/about-nlrb/rights-we-protect/your-rights/your-rights-to-discuss-wages#:~:text=Under%20the%20National%20Labor%20Relations,the%20media%2C%20and%20the%20public.

this is the case, it's likely a company you shouldn't be working for, and you should ask yourself why this discussion is discouraged. The answer is pretty straightforward: it's nearly impossible for employees to call attention to differences in pay if they are not having these discussions with coworkers.

## The Workforce and Women: What's at Stake

I've already spent a lot of time talking about disparities in the workforce, especially as they apply to Black women. My hope is that in the near future, these disparities will no longer exist. For now, though there has been some progress in the gender pay gap, the system is still far from equitable. In this unequal system, it's imperative that we advocate for ourselves on an individual basis because the disparities aren't going to be taken care of for us. It's not fair, but it *is* reality.

There is a pervasive difference in the general philosophy between men and women in the workforce when it comes to pay. Some of this difference is systemically rooted, while some of it stems from beliefs that are ingrained within us as individuals. Either way, it boils down to this: For men, the philosophy seems to be "get paid now and cultivate your credentials down the line." Women, on the other hand, are pushed to prove their credentials first in hopes of getting paid more later, while also not being taught how to negotiate or advocate for their own value.

All this amounts to a staggering loss of income for women—Black women, in particular—over the course of their working lives. According to the National Women's Law Center, women of color lose about $1 million total of pay inequality.[15] With this number in mind, think about how much would change were pay to be equitable. That $1 million spread out over the course of an average forty-year career would allow Black women to afford:

---

15    https://nwlc.org/resource/the-lifetime-wage-gap-state-by-state/.

| | |
|---|---|
| Four-year, in-state tuition at a public university | $104,108 (US average)[16] |
| Five years of groceries for a family of four | $15,588 (USDA moderate food budget for two adults and two kids between six and eight)[17] x 5 = $77,940 |
| Five years of childcare for two school-age children | $4,810[18] (US annual average per child) x 5 = $24,050 x 2 = $48,100 |
| Thirty years of mortgage payments (including insurance, taxes, and fees) | $21,300 (US annual median)[19] x 30-year mortgage term = $639,000 |
| Five years of employee health insurance premiums for one adult | $8,435 (US annual average)[20] x 5 = $42,175 |
| Ten years of utilities (electricity, gas, water, internet, and cell phones) | $6,888 (US household annual average)[21] x 10 = $68,880 |
| Total | $980,203 |

What does this mean? Without the lifetime wage gap, women of color could afford a four-year degree, pay off a thirty-year mortgage to own their home, cover a decade of household utilities, pay five years' worth of health insurance premiums, and feed a family of four for five years while sending two kids to day care.

While the ability to negotiate may not close this $1 million gap, it can help narrow the divide. But just asking for more money isn't

---

16    https://educationdata.org/average-cost-of-college#:~:text=The%20average%20cost%20of%20attendance,or%20%24223%2C360%20over%204%20years.

17    https://www.fns.usda.gov/cnpp/usda-food-plans-cost-food-monthly-reports.

18    https://www.census.gov/library/stories/2024/01/rising-child-care-cost.html.

19    https://www.census.gov/programs-surveys/acs; https://data.census.gov/table/ACSST1Y2022.S2506?q=homeownership.

20    https://www.kff.org/report-section/ehbs-2023-section-1-cost-of-health-insurance/#:~:text=The%20average%20premium%20for%20single,at%20large%20firms%20(%248%2C321).

21    https://www.bankrate.com/mortgages/average-utility-bills/.

enough, even though women have been told that's the reason we make less. It's important to be strategic in these negotiations, especially because we're now as likely as or more likely than men to negotiate our salaries,[22] but still less likely than men to receive an increase.[23] While this is likely driven by a number of factors, some believe that it's a reflection of social norms, which can penalize women for being assertive and negotiating pay, even though men are often rewarded for the same thing.[24] Because cultural norms are difficult to overcome completely in the short term, this is an argument for the importance of pay transparency. It's more difficult for an employer to deny a woman's value when hard numbers for a colleague performing the same job with the same experience are readily available.

In addition to the financial losses that women bear because of gender inequality, it's also important to acknowledge the emotional toll of feeling underpaid and overworked. I don't know about you, but when I've been in these situations, it has made me feel resentful and burnedout. Not only does this negatively impact my experience at work, but it also trickles out to my personal life as well. It is a financial issue, yes, but it's also a quality-of-life issue.

For all these reasons, it's critical that women get comfortable with negotiating their pay. And if you're already negotiating but feel that there's money left on the table, it's time to get more strategic.

## How to Negotiate

It wasn't until I became an entrepreneur that I understood that negotiating wasn't just about getting what I deserved. It was about survival. Entrepreneurship can be unpredictable, and sometimes there is

---

22   https://journals.aom.org/doi/abs/10.5465/amd.2022.0021.

23   https://doi.org/10.1111/irel.12214.

24   https://www.forbes.com/sites/kimelsesser/2023/11/02/women-more-likely-to-negotiate-salaries-but-still-earn-less-than-men-research-says/?sh=186096e7e8b0.

no safety net of a steady paycheck; your success relies on your ability to assert your worth and secure your own income. The "why" when it came to negotiating became clear. There was no backup plan or false sense of job security. No matter how well or badly I performed, there were no longer any guaranteed paychecks from an employer. I was the employer now. This forced me to confront the importance of negotiating for fair pay and favorable terms on my behalf. It was also the realization of my own value as an entrepreneur and an asset in my career field. With each deal I secured and every client I booked, I gained a deeper appreciation for the skills and expertise that I brought to my industry.

When you learn to value yourself, everything changes. When you know your worth and can advocate for yourself, chances are that your financial life will become less stressful and more rewarding. Imagine how much freer and lighter life would feel if you could pay your bills without stressing out or feeling stretched every month. Imagine how secure you could feel if you knew that you were earning enough that you could take care not only of your current needs but also your future needs. Imagine how much easier negotiations and conversations about money would be if you *knew* what you were worth and understood how to speak to that. Imagine feeling like you were being compensated and respected as you should be in the workplace.

The time to have these negotiations is now, even if you consider your current position temporary. Compound interest starts today. Don't make the mistake of assuming that you can start fresh at your next job, because your current salary likely sets the bar for the salary at the next job. And if you're going to stay where you are, your future raises are dictated by how you negotiate your salary today. You are doing more than just solving a short-term problem, you're setting the tone for the future.

Before we get into the nuts and bolts of salary conversations, I want you to know this: negotiation doesn't have to be a battle between you and your employer. Some of us are under the impression that negotiation is somehow combative, but this is not the case at all. It's a conversation grounded in fact, and it's likely a conversation that your employer is used to having—and even anticipates. Negotiation is a learned skill, and the more you practice, the easier it will be. There is a way to advocate for yourself in a professional setting, and I'm going to show you how.

## Track Your Success

Aside from the importance of tracking accomplishments so that you can articulate and quantify them for your employer, I've found that writing down successes goes a long way to understanding your value as well. This kind of recordkeeping is helpful in negotiations and a powerful tool for confronting and overcoming the internalized beliefs that can hold me back when it comes to advocating for myself. If you track your accomplishments, it reinforces the fact that you are an asset not only to the company you work for, but also to every table at which you sit. This understanding allows you to interview, negotiate, and advance in your career with a greater sense of self-worth and ease.

Begin making a habit of tracking all your responsibilities and achievements on a regular basis. Don't assume that you will remember this information over time. Track and log each success, achievement, and milestone, and make note of every time that you go beyond your job function and do more, thus increasing your value to the company. Note the differentiators that make you particularly effective at completing this work successfully. For example, consider your strong problem-solving skills, expertise in project management, ability to analyze complex data, effective collaboration with team members, or talent for strategic planning. Document the milestones you've achieved with the company. Take note of your significant accomplishments, such as leading successful cross-functional initiatives, exceeding performance targets, or any recognition you've received from upper management.

This is only the first step, though, because understanding your value is one thing; being able to articulate it is something else entirely, and it's a skill you must cultivate in order to negotiate. This means more than just listing things you've done and accomplished; it means understanding and then communicating the *impact* of this work on the company's overall goals and success. Remember that companies speak the language of the bottom line, so whenever possible, try to gain an understanding of the impact your work and achievements have had on your employer's overall goals and success.

Think of this as presenting your achievements in a format that speaks directly to the company's success. For example, "I implemented a new marketing strategy that increased our website traffic by 25 percent [the accomplishment], resulting in a 20 percent increase in online sales [the results]." Or "I revamped our customer service procedures [the accomplishment], reducing response times by 50 percent, which led to a 22 percent increase in customer satisfaction rating and rise in customer retention [the results]."

## Know Your Number

Now that you know why you deserve a raise, it's time to think about what that increase should be so that you can be specific in your request. One common mistake I see is women who come to a negotiation with all their accomplishments and successes in hand but leave it up to the employer to determine what that's worth. It's important that you go into the negotiation with a number in mind, because whoever throws down the first number sets the tone for the negotiation, and chances are your employer will start with a lower number than you will. Sometimes it's helpful to pick a range rather than one hard number. This allows you some wiggle room during discussions by starting at the upper end of your range without painting yourself into a corner.

Coming up with a number that you're likely to attain requires knowing two things:

1 The average salary for your role, accounting for factors like location (which impacts cost of living), industry, and the amount of experience you have in that sector.
2 Your own personal financial needs.

## Gather Comparable Salary Information

Your market value depends on your job title and industry, your education and years of experience, any specific skills or advanced certificates, and your geographic location. The US Bureau of Labor Statistics provides wage data for over eight hundred occupations and by state.[25] You can also try out online tools to calculate your going market rate on sites like Glassdoor[26] and PayScale.[27] These tools allow you to enter your specific information to get an idea of the salary you should ask for. Doing this basic market research ahead of time will allow you to walk into any negotiations as prepared as possible.

As you look for information on comparable roles, focus on similar industries. For example, an administrative assistant or project manager in the tech industry will likely make a significantly higher salary than the same role at a nonprofit. Not only will solid data like this help you come up with an appropriate number and justify it to your employer, but it also helps get you into a logical frame of mind for the negotiation, as opposed to an emotional one. You are presenting facts here, and, unlike emotion, facts leave little room for debate.

As we've discussed, talking about salary and wages with coworkers can feel delicate. At best, it's awkward to broach these conversations

---

25   https://www.bls.gov/bls/blswage.htm.
26   Ibid.
27   https://www.payscale.com/.

that most of us have been trained not to have. But it's also important, because once you understand how much your colleagues earn, you will be in a much better position to understand your own market value. And remember, these conversations potentially help them as well. When having these conversations, you'll want to identify a colleague whose role is as comparable to yours as possible: they perform the same function, have a similar background, and have faced similar challenges and experiences in the workplace.

When you are preparing to talk to your colleagues, it's important to be positive and open-minded to set the tone for a productive conversation. Make sure you pick a good time and place where you can talk without any interruptions and minimize distractions. During the conversation, be clear and direct about what you want to talk about. Begin by acknowledging their work ethic, expertise, and strengths and your reasoning for pulling them to the side. Then express your interest in understanding how your salaries compare and emphasize that you value transparency and fairness in compensation. Be direct but considerate in your approach, explaining your reasons for wanting to discuss salary comparison, but understand and respect their right to decline. While sharing your own salary may be uncomfortable, consider disclosing your information first if it could facilitate a more open discussion. Throughout the conversation, maintain professionalism and confidentiality. This isn't a competition or confrontation; this is a conversation focused on collaboration to promote fair compensation.

In some cases, you may not be able to have direct conversations with your colleagues. You can approach the topic indirectly by sharing industry data and asking for their opinion about how the company meets those standards. For example, "Hey, I was talking to a friend who is in a similar role at another company, and they mentioned how they negotiated their salary by comparing salaries in our field. It got me curious about how our salaries here measure up against industry

numbers. Have you ever thought about using industry data to negotiate your salary?" Another example could look like sharing an article with your team and saying, "I read an article about how different
companies pay people differently for the same job. What do you think
about that?" These conversation starters are subtle, making it easy for
everyone involved to engage in the conversation without being pres-
sured or uncomfortable.

## Know Your Financial Goals

When considering the second factor, your own financial needs, I encourage you to think beyond your current monthly expenses for all the
reasons we've discussed throughout this book. Think not just of Current You, but also Future You. This isn't about just putting yourself
into a better position to pay your rent, but to someday buy a house,
grow a family, educate your children, or even just get to a place where
you have more disposable income. Sure, you might not accomplish
all that with one raise, but remember: each negotiation sets the tone
for future negotiations and gets you that much closer to where you
want to be. There are no absolute rules on how much of an increase
you should ask for, whether it's a percentage of your current salary or
a specific dollar increase. However, as a first step, you can aim for a
salary that aligns with your market value and the value you bring to
the company.

No matter how prepared you are, being scared or nervous is totally
normal. Here are some things to keep in mind:

## Negotiation Extends Beyond Salary

Negotiations don't have to feel like a confrontation. Go in knowing
your worth and be prepared to share your research and personal accomplishments.

Sometimes, however, no matter how deserving you are, there simply isn't any money in the budget to increase your salary. Ask ques-

tions about how your managers have arrived at your salary or if there are any company-wide barriers to your request, such as hiring freezes. Remember there are other perks of potential value beyond additional money in your paycheck. For example, if you work at a company that's located in a high-traffic area but doesn't offer free parking, you might negotiate discounted parking or public transportation. While this isn't more money in your paycheck per se, it does save you from paying for ongoing expenses, which frees up more money for you to spend in other areas.

Other perks might include flexible working hours, professional development opportunities, or specialized training. Maybe your company makes a higher contribution to your health care. Get creative and think about things that would hold value to you, whether strictly financial or not.

## Practice

Even with all this information on your side, it's completely normal to feel intimidated at the thought of the actual conversation. To alleviate jitters and gain some experience negotiating, I highly recommend that you get some practice under your belt by asking friends, family, or even a trusted coworker who has been in the same situation as you to sit down with you for mock negotiations. Everyone should practice negotiating, but it's particularly important if you're someone who's not used to celebrating your own accomplishments. Speaking them aloud to someone who already understands your worth and can call you out when you're undermining yourself will help you break the habit of downplaying your successes. Otherwise, this conditioning can really hurt women when it comes to moving up in the workplace. Even if you feel silly, mock negotiations help you practice responding to different reactions, facial expressions, silence, or an initial "no" so you can keep the discussion going. The more you practice doing this, the more natural it will become.

Although we've been discussing negotiations in terms of salary increases in this chapter, negotiation and self-advocacy are a part of all our lives in many other ways too. You negotiate and advocate when you're buying a car, discussing terms with contractors for home renovations, deciding where to go for dinner with your friends, assigning household chores to your family, resolving conflicts, setting relationship boundaries, or planning vacations.

Become extra present the next time you find yourself in one of these situations. Notice how you hold yourself—are you sitting straight or slouching? Relaxed or rigid? Speaking with confidence or muttering? Claiming your space or making yourself small? Notice what does and doesn't work. Consciously focus on building this muscle, learning from both your wins and losses, adjusting and refining your skills every chance you get. Also, use negotiations in other parts of your life as an opportunity to notice that you *can* do this, even if you haven't yet exercised this skill in the workplace.

Of course, we hope that all negotiations play out how we want them to—but chances are they won't. It's helpful to be in situations where you receive pushback so that you know how to handle them better in the future.

## Consider the Timing

Armed with information and practice under your belt, it's time to set up a meeting with the appropriate person at your company. For best results, be thoughtful about the timing of your conversation. Consider aligning your request with the performance review period. This creates a strategic opportunity to discuss your achievements and contributions to the company.

Try to assess the company's financial health beforehand. This may take a little legwork on your end to find this information, but it would be best to avoid asking for raises during financial difficulties and budget freezes. Time your request around personal milestones or after completing a big project that can help make for a strong argument. Research the market to learn more about the current demand for your skills, because that can also help with timing and competition in the market. You want to get familiar with the culture and norms of negotiations in your company. This doesn't mean you have to fall in line with any unfair practices, but you should be aware of how things work.

Timing extends beyond just what's happening at your company and also to what's happening in the industry. You'll want to keep your pulse on developments within your field so that you're aware when things are shifting or changing to your benefit. For example, let's say you're a nurse, and there's currently a nurse shortage. How can you use that to your advantage when it comes to negotiations? How might it make you more valuable? Or maybe you see an increased demand for digital marketing and know you have expertise that others don't. This puts you in a strong position to negotiate a new role, or even ask for more money in your current position, because your employer will understand you can easily go elsewhere, and those other companies are likely willing to pay more for your services.

If I haven't yet convinced you of the importance of advocating for yourself in the workplace, consider this: How do you feel right now? If you know that you aren't making enough money, deserve more, and feel unrecognized, I'm willing to bet you have some feelings about this. On top of all the other things I struggled with when I wasn't making enough money, I also consistently felt unhappy and bitter. Every time I paid a bill or went to the grocery store, I was reminded of the fact that I was working simply to survive. And that didn't feel good. It impacted my experience at work, and it also impacted my overall quality of life outside work.

No matter how intimidated you might feel about negotiation—it's worth it. Even if you walk away from the table without getting what you'd hoped for, a negative response can illuminate your next step and arm you with more negotiating skills in the future.

While it's important that you assume responsibility for making your voice heard when it comes to fair compensation, the system as it stands *is* unfair and inequitable to women. Larger change needs to happen. But until then, a win for each woman is a win for all of us as we normalize asking for what we're worth.

## Negotiation Checklist

Best times to ask for more:

- During salary negotiations for any new job
- During a performance review, or once a year if you don't have regular reviews
- If you've achieved specific goals or significant achievements
- When you're offered a promotion
- Anytime you're asked to take on significantly more responsibility even when it comes without an official new title
- If you've completed advanced training or education, or added a new skill or certification
- If you learn that colleagues are paid more than you for the same work
- If the market rate you researched is significantly higher than your salary/wage
- When you've been offered a job at another company

What to do before negotiations:

- Know your worth—Track your successes and know your market rate
- Practice and prepare—Reduce nervous energy with mock interviews
- Set up for success—Choose the right timing, contact person, and setting

What to do during negotiations:

- Be specific—Ask for the number aligned with your financial goals
- Be confident—Share your success metrics and achievements to support your ask
- Be flexible—Consider salary/wage increases along with other perks such as flexible working hours or education stipend

# CHAPTER 12

# My Final Love Letter (Generational Wealth)

The morning of December 19, 2017, I'd gone to work after dropping off my kids at day care as usual. Around lunchtime I received several calls from a number I didn't recognize, so I didn't pick up the first few times, but the person on the other end of the line was persistent. I clocked out for lunch and finally picked up the phone when the same unknown number flashed across my screen. I was surprised to hear it was my stepmother, but her voice sounded all wrong when she asked if I was sitting down. When she told me my dad had passed away, I remember my phone slipping from my hand and hitting the floor, but only because I remember what shoes I had on that day. I remember screaming, but only because I remember my mouth opening and the look on my friend's face, who was also my coworker, when she heard the noise come out of my mouth, but I don't recall the sound I made. A coworker who'd been somewhat of a grandmother figure to me grabbed my hands and told me to pull myself together because I needed to deal with this emergency and still make it home to my children safely at the end of the day. I went to my father's house, straight from the office.

"Daddy tried, baby." Dad's voice rang in my ears as I sat in his bedroom waiting for the coroner. I looked around to see all his attempts at survival. He'd been trying to hook up his CPAP machine. His inhalers were strewn across the bed. It was clear to me that my dad was trying to fight for his life, and the only thing that brought me comfort was remembering whenever I heard him say those words growing up. It was my dad's shorthand for saying he'd exhausted all options and done everything in his power and fell short. My father's relentless efforts, even in the face of financial difficulties, to provide and care for me, and his ultimate struggle for life itself, embody the essence of parental love and responsibility.

"Daddy tried, baby" highlights parents' inherent desire to do everything within their power to make sure of the well-being and security of their children, even when faced with overwhelming or inevitable challenges, like illness and death. Although my dad passed away suddenly without a will in place and no instructions on how to access his information or any benefits, I know he did the best he could with what he had.

We got a small break thanks to a kind representative at his company who allowed us to guess his life insurance beneficiaries. Although my dad never took out life insurance on his own, his employer luckily offered a policy, and we were able to access a $10,000 payout to cover part of the funeral expenses. We still had many out-of-pocket expenses and a difficult time accessing all his information so we could properly close out all his accounts, obtain paperwork, and settle his small estate.

I can accept that my dad's sudden passing meant he left his family without communicating his last wishes and, at the same time, want to do better for my kids, especially because I remember how hard it was to grieve my dad while having to take care of all the funeral arrangements. Beyond those logistics, I've made peace with the fact that my parents, especially my dad, were unable to focus on generational wealth. But they certainly did everything they could to build the foundation for me.

My parents grew up in a low-income household in a low-income community and were teenagers when I was born. We were much closer to generational poverty than even the idea of generational wealth. Every penny my parents earned went toward the immediate needs of our family, with nothing left over to put to the side for the future. This same cycle continued when I also became a mother at an early age. The financial blueprint provided to me was a plan of survival, not wealth building.

Standard conversations about generational wealth, like investing in real estate and the stock market or passing down a lucrative family business, were irrelevant to me. Putting money aside for future generations meant taking from the current one, and that was something that my parents couldn't afford. And neither could I. Generational wealth was a narrative that belonged to other people. It was something I only read about in books or watched in movies with characters that were already superrich and living in mansions with children in private schools being prepped to take over the multimillion-dollar family business. Generational wealth was a story for those with the means and resources completely different from my own or anyone I knew.

## Building Generational Wealth Your Way

As a parent, I always thought about my children's future and what I could do to break the cycle that my great-grandma, grandma, mom, and I were trapped in. As I navigated my own financial challenges as a single mom simply trying to make it through the day, I had a realization about generational wealth: it is not a monolith. It did not have to come in the form of real estate enterprises, large stock portfolios, or multimillion-dollar businesses. It could be anything—monetary or nonmonetary—

that paved a smoother way for the generation following mine, in my case, my children. It made me think about all the nonmonetary ways I'd seen my grandparents support my parents and, in turn, help them save money for our immediate needs and future savings.

After school we spent time with my grandma while we waited for my mom to get off work before going home. Considering the average cost of childcare today, my parents would have had to pay hundreds or even thousands of dollars per month for four children. It's fair to say that my grandma assisting my parents with childcare helped them avoid an extra expense that probably would have had a domino effect on their ability to make ends meet. My grandma's contribution was an investment in our family's financial stability, and while it did not increase the number in my parents' bank accounts directly, this act exemplifies how generational support, a nonmonetary transaction, can manifest itself in a way that directly impacts our financial well-being.

Looking at generational wealth this way allowed me to enter this conversation on my own terms and see that many of my efforts, though not immediately lucrative, were still deposits being made for a brighter future. This has led me to my belief that generational wealth is not just an accumulation of assets but also the transmission of knowledge, support, skills, and the spirit of perseverance and re-silience. Honestly, that's worth more than anything else when it's the only option you have.

## Generational Wealth Is About More than Money

Generational wealth takes just that to build—generations.

There may not be many people in our generation who can pass down millions of dollars or dozens of properties. Still, you can do inexpensive yet impactful things over time to alleviate some financial barriers.

In these situations, it's hard not to let your net worth define your self-worth, but it's super important to distinguish the two so we can have healthier relationships with money and build generational wealth in our own ways. Progress takes time, and we may have assets that don't immediately transfer to wealth in a way that it changes our net worth, but that doesn't mean they're not valuable.

Whether you help your sister improve her résumé so she can get a higher-paying job, give your young cousin rides to work so they can save money on transportation, or teach your grandparents how to avoid internet scams, it's never just about direct financial support. Of course, you're helping your loved ones save money, earn more, or avoid debt, but you're also laying the foundation for generational stability and growth within your family. By providing practical, emotional, and mental support, you create a ripple effect, where each small act makes it easier for the next generation to reach higher levels of education and employment, thus increasing their potential to contribute to the family's wealth. You're also modeling individual, family, and community care, resulting in deeper connections and a secure network of mutual aid.

From teaching young adults financial literacy or a profitable skill to getting life insurance, setting up investment accounts, or teaching your kids to budget and negotiate their salary, it all makes a difference. What we often forget is that these acts of care and support aren't really about the money, just like our connections and relationships can't be reduced to transactions.

While grieving the sudden loss of my dad, I sat across from the funeral director with $600 in cash, buying a burial plot. As I handed over the bills, she filled out a receipt. I looked at the receipt in my hands, reflecting on how my father had lived a whole life, and all of it came down to this financial transaction.

I still have that piece of paper today. It reminds me that building generational wealth isn't just about financial security, but making our children feel cared for and loved emotionally and mentally as well. Generational wealth is about mutual aid and a strong sense of community. It's about taking the positives from the generations before and building upon them, then teaching our kids to do the same.

Giving generational support is not "coddling." We need to find a balance between our country's ideals of mutual aid and rugged individualism. I believe in a healthy combination of providing loving support while teaching responsibility and independence. My young cousins, niece, and other members of my family know that I back up my advice with results. They see what I've accomplished, so my recommendations hold weight. Plus, I'm not afraid to hold their hands as I guide them into adulthood. It can be a tough transition for anyone, especially young adults between eighteen and twenty-five. Hell, I'm in my mid-thirties, and finances are still scary for me to navigate at times.

## Generational Wealth Is Multidirectional

Generational wealth moves up and down and sideways. We often think of grandparents or parents passing down wealth to their kids and grandkids. However, generational wealth can also move upward and across families and generations. This multidirectional flow of resources, knowledge, and money allows all members of the family to contribute and benefit from the collective wealth regardless of generation. Why is this important? Shared responsibility. It can look like grandparents investing in their grandchildren, parents supporting their children, aunts and uncles helping out their nieces. With this "all hands on deck" approach, we can create a sense of mutual responsibility and support that reduces financial stress on the current working generation.

For example, the pandemic hit the millennials in my family, who currently carry the majority of the financial weight, extremely hard, and we faced a ton of financial challenges. During that time, support came from both the older and younger generations to help ease the stress and provide a financial safety net.

**Downward flow**—This is the most common form of generational wealth we see, where parents pass down assets, values, and knowledge directly to their children and then to their grandchildren. The goal here is usually to provide the next generation with a better starting point than the previous one.

**Upward flow**—When generational wealth moves upward, we are supporting the older generations, usually parents and grandparents, which isn't uncommon but not necessarily considered generational wealth building. This can look like financial support to help the older generation with retirement or healthcare costs, or any nonmonetary support like providing senior care, help with physical chores, rides to the doctor or social activities, or assisting with technology. And of course, keeping our elders safe from the newest phone or email scams!

**Cross flow**—Generational wealth can also move sideways. I'm the oldest sibling and oldest daughter, and I know firsthand how our money can be used to support siblings, cousins, and other family members of the same generation. This can take on many forms, but here are some ways my siblings and I have supported each other:

- My brother using his college degree in communications to assist me with media training, content creation, and public speaking
- My sister saving me money by doing my hair and makeup for speaking engagements
- My youngest sister acting as my personal assistant during the early stages of building my business
- Teaching my cousins how to budget and start investment accounts
- Teaching my siblings how to create résumés and negotiate salaries

Not everything we do puts cash into other people's pockets, but these actions can be impactful enough to change the trajectory of our finances. This shows how all family members have something valuable to contribute, regardless of their age and financial status. It's our opportunity to dive deeper into generational wealth so that everyone can participate in it.

It's essential to balance everyday small acts with the foundational strategies that will provide long-term financial opportunities and security for yourself, your kids, and your extended family. My experience in the wake of my dad's death underscores the importance of extending our efforts beyond our death by leaving a living legacy in the form of what I call a *final love letter*—a comprehensive document detailing how your assets will be distributed after your death. What if you're not a parent yet or have no plans to have children? Do you still need this document? Yes! You don't need a child as your primary motivation to improve your finances, create a living legacy, and allocate your assets in the most meaningful way to you. Your final love letter can help you put your affairs in order regardless of who will benefit from the wealth you build. Maybe you want to make plans for a beloved pet, a charity close to your heart, or dear friends and extended family members.

## Your Final Love Letter— Your Legacy for Building Wealth

After struggling to locate my dad's financial information when he passed away, I prepared a "final love letter" for my kids. I see this comprehensive financial document as a final act of love from a parent to her children rather than just a list of who gets what. Of course, this final love letter helps ensure that your family is taken care of after your death, but it's so much more. By outlining your wishes and values, you can guide and support your family during a difficult time and help avoid unnecessary financial stress and conflict. This is the way to build generational wealth beyond your death.

It's important to keep this final love letter in a safe place and update it as needed, such as if you get divorced, have another child, or open new accounts. Make sure your attorney and several trusted people—your spouse, sibling, or best friend—know where to find this information.

## Here's What I Included in My Final Love Letter and Why:

**Letter of instruction**—Outlines your wishes for how assets should be managed and distributed after your death.

As a mom, it's tough to think about the day that I'm no longer able to physically take care of my children. I find peace in knowing that I'm doing everything humanly possible to care for them long after I'm gone. The letter of instruction is one of the most basic documents to ensure that this will happen to my exact specifications.

**Will**—Foundational document for how your assets will be distributed after your death, spelling out in detail what's been outlined in your letter of instruction.

A will is essential for single parents, because it also gives you a voice in the courtroom even when you're not physically present, ensuring that your choices for a guardian of your children will be considered.

**Healthcare directive**—A document detailing your preferences for medical care decisions in the event you're incapacitated and can no longer make these decisions yourself.

You may be most familiar with "Do Not Resuscitate" (DNR) requests, but these advanced directives or "living wills" can include anything from whether you want to donate your organs, what types of life-prolonging or -sustaining treatments you accept or deny, which tests you want done or which drugs to avoid. You can also name a trusted individual to make decisions on your behalf or enforce the healthcare directive.

**Estate plan**—Comprehensive plan for how assets will be managed and distributed during your lifetime and after death.

An estate plan usually includes a will but is a more in-depth plan comprised of additional financial documents, such as trusts or healthcare directives in case you're incapacitated by an injury or illness. An estate plan also allows you to minimize tax payments so more of your assets go to the beneficiaries you selected.

**Guardianship**—Legal arrangement for who will take care of your kids when you can no longer.

This is one of the most important decisions you will include in your final love letter, the direct emotional, physical, and financial care of your children. Parental preference has a lot of weight when a court decides on a child's guardian, but of course they will determine if the selected guardian is fit to provide a stable, loving, and safe environment for the child and is willing to take on the responsibility.

**Prenup**—Can specify that assets are intended for children from a previous marriage or relationship.

A prenup can be a complement to your estate plan, especially if you and your partner have children together and from previous relationships and marriages. You'll want to be very clear about which of your assets go to your new spouse and each of the children.

**Life insurance**—A policy that pays a sum of money upon your death to cover funeral expenses, outstanding debts, and support for your loved ones.

For the longest time, I avoided getting life insurance out of the fearful superstition that I would be "speaking death" over me and my family. This perspective on death, that discussing it would invite bad luck, is common across many cultures. Working in the insurance industry and seeing the benefits of people preparing for something as unavoidable as death and experiencing the sudden loss of my father changed my attitude. In this book and across my platforms, I'm now committed to breaking the cultural taboos on planning for death because I learned firsthand how important these conversations are.

The day I purchased life insurance for my children, I cried while signing the paperwork. It was one of the most emotional financial tasks I've had to complete as an adult. Just the thought of my children having to deal with losing me like I lost my dad was heartbreaking. I just had to sit with the anger and sadness while going through the process because I knew it was the right thing to do for my kids. Many parents spend their entire lives trying to "figure it out" and "make it big," but then they die and leave their children with nothing but broken promises and empty accounts. Getting life insurance is emotionally draining but one of the most affordable ways to set your kids up with a financial cushion during an intense period of grief and loss. The truth is, we don't have forever, and life can suddenly change at a moment's notice. The sudden loss of a primary income can cripple an entire family for generations.

When considering how much life insurance to take out, a general recommendation is to calculate for ten–fifteen times your income so all your current bills are covered, including household expenses such as groceries and utility bills, medical costs for treatments and prescriptions, and personal expenses such as extracurriculars or tuition. If you have any debt, including car loans or mortgages, you need to factor in those payments so your children don't lose transportation or housing. You also need to consider how long your life insurance coverage should last. Ideally, you'll want to cover your longest debt (say, a thirty-year mortgage).

Life insurance is an ultimate display of love and says to your children: "In my death, I will give you what I couldn't have while alive." It's a harsh reality for many parents. I consider it one of the primary, and most accessible, ways to ensure financial security for your children.

### Retirement accounts—401(k)s or IRAs

It's important to designate the beneficiaries of your retirement accounts, including alternative options (in case your original beneficiaries die before you or can't inherit the accounts for unforeseen reasons). In many cases, spouses are automatically considered the primary beneficiaries, so if you want to leave your assets to someone else, you better spell out your wishes exactly. You'll also need to take into consideration what tax implications will result for each of your beneficiaries. An attorney specializing in estate planning can help you figure out the complexities.

**Education funding**—Savings policies for educational expenses, including college.

The most common savings plan parents can start for their kids' college education is a 529 plan or an Educational Savings Account (ESA). I started 529 plans for my kids, but both types of educational savings plans can be used for primary and secondary education (K–12 and college). These two main options have different tax advantages, annual contribution limits, income restrictions, and withdrawal policies, plus the 529 can vary by state, so it's important you review the fine print. Your employer may also sponsor education assistance for your kids as part of their employee benefits package.

**Power of attorney**—Legal authorization for someone to act on your behalf in financial or medical matters.

The person you select can be a family member, friend, spouse, or an actual attorney. This person can make financial and healthcare decisions, as well as legal transactions on your behalf. They can operate your business, manage your real estate, or be tasked with any other specific roles and responsibilities to perform in the event you're incapacitated. It's important to remember that a POA automatically ends when you die, at which point the person you named executor of your will takes over. Of course, you can choose the same person for both.

Creating a final love letter can be emotionally draining, but you'll be glad for the peace of mind it creates for you and your family in the future. Learning to develop financial security for myself means I'm much more likely to build a living legacy of financial and emotional wealth for my kids.

My dad did the best he could with what he had before he passed, and my mom continues to do so every day. It's my honor to carry on my parents' legacy as long as I live. I'm dedicated to learning from my parents' struggles so I can do a little better for my kids, and I hope that my kids will learn from my challenges and do better for their kids, and so on. Ultimately, building generational wealth by creating a living legacy is not just about money and assets but consistent support, guidance, and empowerment that will enable future generations to thrive and succeed. By finding creative ways to support the younger generation in our families, we can help build a brighter future for everyone.

## Final Love Letter—Checklist

Steps to take when you create your legacy of love:

1. Create these financial documents with an attorney or have them notarized to make sure they'll be enforceable should something happen to you.

2. Update your documents, beneficiaries, accounts, and final love letter after major life events, such as a wedding or divorce, the birth of a child or death of a beneficiary, or receiving an inheritance.

3. Reduce your debt as much as possible to avoid your children being saddled with it after your death. Generally, kids aren't responsible for parents' debts, but you may have cosigned loans, hold joint accounts, or leave your child a house that's in foreclosure.

Topics to consider for inclusion in your final love letter:

- **Letter of instruction**—Outlines your wishes for how assets should be managed and distributed after your death.
- **Will**—Foundational document for how your assets will be distributed after your death, spelling out in detail what's been outlined in your letter of instruction.
- **Healthcare directive**—A document detailing your preferences for medical care decisions in the event you're incapacitated and can no longer make these decisions yourself.
- **Estate plan**—Comprehensive plan for how assets will be managed and distributed during your lifetime and after death. An estate plan usually includes a will and additional financial documents such as trusts or healthcare directives.

- **Guardianship**—Legal arrangement for who will take care of your kids when you can no longer.
- **Prenup**—Can specify that assets are intended for children from a previous marriage or relationship. A prenup can be a complement to your estate plan, especially if you and your partner have children together and from previous relationships and marriages.
- **Life insurance**—A policy that pays a sum of money upon your death to cover funeral expenses, outstanding debts, and support for your loved ones. I consider it one of the primary, and most accessible, ways to ensure financial security for your children.
- **Retirement accounts**—401(k)s or IRAs, as well as education funding / 529 plans. It's important to designate the beneficiaries of your retirement accounts, including alternative options in case your original beneficiaries die before you or can't inherit the accounts for unforeseen reasons.
- **Power of attorney**—Legal authorization for someone to act on your behalf in financial or medical matters. The person you select can be a family member, friend, spouse, or an actual attorney.

# The Power of Perseverance in Personal Finance

**M**omma, why do you have those sandals on when it's cold outside?" my son asked me eight years ago, during an ad on his favorite YouTube channel. As quickly as he asked me this, the ad was over and he was back to watching his show, oblivious to the weight he had just dropped on me. I could feel my eyes welling with tears while we walked down the street to his day care after getting off the bus. I kept my head slightly lifted to avoid the tears from running down my face. This was one of the most innocent yet gut-wrenching questions one of my sons had ever asked me.

It was toward the end of fall, and it was one of the toughest times of the year for me as a single mom. Fall was challenging because it came right after I spent any extra money on getting my oldest son ready for back to school—new uniforms, shoes, and supplies. By November of every year, I'd spent every dime I'd had on school supplies and bills and worked tirelessly during the summer, so much so that the seasons changed faster than my money could keep up.

I didn't realize until that very moment that I'd been wearing the same pair of bronze open-toed sandals since the summer. During this time, I was also going through my divorce, which financially drained me. His question made me realize how much I had been sacrificing and how visible those sacrifices were to my children, no matter how I tried to hide them. At the time, I let out a slight chuckle at his innocent inquiry, but it was an eye-opener for me and a realization of how closely our children pay attention to the decisions we make. At his age, he would not have been able to comprehend that I simply did not have the extra money to buy a new pair of shoes and was trying to hold out, hoping to beat the dropping temperature for a few more weeks before receiving an expected bonus. I had prioritized their needs so high above my own that I didn't even notice the chill on my toes.

This moment was less about the physical discomfort of wearing sandals in cold weather but more about the sacrifices and decisions I had to make to prioritize my children's needs over my own. Here I was again, continuing to push forward with limited resources and making tough choices in the face of personal and financial hardship. That question lit a fire under me and set off a determination to work even harder, to persevere, and to move beyond being broke. This type of perseverance is what thousands of women tap into daily.

Perseverance in personal finance for women means consistently taking steps toward financial security, despite the challenges and barriers that we may face. From having to wear the same pair of shoes during the changing seasons to working multiple jobs to make ends meet, perseverance is about finding the strength to keep going. It means being determined to keep pushing through obstacles, even when it feels like progress is slow or nonexistent. When I look back on my life and my experience with money, every moment tells the story of perseverance, a battle against the visible and invisible barriers to financial stability and wealth, many of which I had no control over. But this isn't just my story. I share these feelings with thousands of women from different backgrounds who meet at the intersection of gender, race, and economic inequality.

For years, the power of perseverance was the most valuable and only asset I owned when I began my personal finance journey. It wasn't just a concept; it was a daily practice in my life made through small actions and decisions. Without a car, public transportation was my lifeline. I woke up before dawn, leaving the house while it was still dark during the week to catch the first of several buses to get to work. This journey was long—two hours one way on two different buses. Four hours of my day were spent in transit to make sure my children had food on the table. There were many times when my financial resources were stretched so thin that I had to use dollar stores and sales just to stretch the food budget, intentionally overdraw my bank account just to get gas in between pay periods, repair clothes instead of buying new ones, or sleep in one bedroom with my children with an electric heater during the winter to avoid a ridiculously high heating bill. Yet somehow I managed our household budget, often deciding between necessities while making sure essential bills were paid. I sought higher education to increase my income despite my financial and time constraints. I failed several times and dropped out, but I was determined to improve our situation. When I ran into unexpected expenses that had the potential to derail my finances entirely, the small $5 and $10 I put aside over time became the small cushion I desperately needed. Perseverance in personal finance isn't just about enduring hardships but actively finding ways to overcome them. **Still, these hardships taught me that, while we may not have control over our circumstances, we do have control over how we respond to them.**

## Being a Woman Is Expensive

I grew up in a matriarch-led family, and our perseverance was not only about survival but also about securing a better future for ourselves and the generations to follow. Not only do women typically have to make day-to-day financial decisions, but they also have to teach and pass on lessons that go beyond just making ends meet and basic survival skills. We are often left with the responsibility of teaching lessons on resilience, strategy, and the art of making a dollar out of fifteen cents. It's what my grandmother taught my mother, and it's what my mother taught me. This became the foundation on which I built my financial identity.

It instilled in me the understanding that, despite how little I had, financial knowledge can be life-changing and that each decision we make, no matter how small, can have a major impact on our future. But this commitment to persevere through financial difficulties is not a new concept. It's important to recognize that there has never been a time when Black women did not *push forward*. This narrative is deeply intertwined with the history of Black women and money, highlighting the progress we've made and the challenges we still face. In the earlier chapters, we talked about how historically women were relegated to one segment of the household: homemaking, with little to no control over household finances. As we moved into the twentieth century, we saw that dynamic start to shift as a result of different Black and women-centered movements that transitioned women from homemakers to contributors and, increasingly, to primary breadwinners. Throughout history, Black women have often been the backbone of their families and communities, working both inside and outside the home.

And yet, I want to acknowledge that while perseverance and survival have been necessary to women's financial journeys, those traits should not define our experiences. We should not have to endure, get knocked down, and get back up over and over again. It's unfair that the financial deck has been stacked against us, making these traits necessary for survival. The reality is that these barriers have not only shaped our financial struggles but also forced us to constantly prove our resilience. **While perseverance is celebrated, it should not be a** requirement for financial stability. Women deserve to engage in the financial world without the added burden of having to constantly overcome adversity.

Almost every hardship that has occurred in my life traces back to one thing—money or the lack thereof—even before I was born. My mother was born into a low-income family who lived in a multigenerational house owned by my great-grandmother. When I was born, my grandmother made me a bassinet out of a dresser drawer. This was a result of a lack of space and resources, but she decided to make do with what was available. My mom was a teenager when she gave birth to me, which affected her education and employment and, in return, determined where we lived, the school I was able to attend, all the way down to the food we could afford to eat—three major factors that have been scientifically linked to the development of a child. After my mother and father separated when I was eleven, I witnessed my mom work tirelessly to improve our lives by trying to increase her income at the same rate that our expenses increased.

As the oldest child and oldest daughter, the call on me to be more hands on with my siblings was immediate, and as I entered my teens, this also affected where I worked and where I attended school. The cycle repeated itself. Had my grandmother had the financial resources she needed, my mother would've had the resources she needed, and I would have had the resources I needed and ultimately been able to curb some of the financial hardships my children and I encountered.

Originally, I believed my financial journey started at the age of nineteen, but in reality, it started almost a half century before I got here. Financial inequality starts early for women, from being paid differently for chores all the way up to being paid differently for the same job as our male counterparts, and this doesn't take into account the significant inequalities that surround motherhood and marriage. Women having access to financial resources goes beyond bank accounts or being able to afford material items. When women have money, the entire economy benefits. I'm not referring to the tired and old stereotypes that women are shopaholics or exhaust most of our money on beauty products; those are lazy takes used as a distraction from the bigger picture. I'm referring to the underlying issues that impact women and exist within the infrastructure of the financial systems across the world.

**Again, being a woman is expensive.** That is more than just a statement. That is a lived reality. It's measured in the pink tax, the gender pay gap, healthcare and reproductive costs, gender-based discriminatory prices, the high risk of career interruptions for childcare, the retirement savings gap, and the invisible, unpaid household labor and childcare we take on.

And women are not the only ones paying the price. The economic costs associated with gender pay inequality are steep. Because women are the primary caretakers of families, making less and having higher expenses affects the financial stability of extended families. Because we have limited access to resources, such as unequal educational and career opportunities, the resulting loss of our talent and productivity further hurts the country's economy. The financial stress of all this causes depression, anxiety, and other mental health problems that make it even harder to hold down jobs while taking care of everyone else, like a vehicle running on fumes. The financial burden of being a woman extends beyond individual problems and impacts everyone, our families, communities, and society as a whole, making it that much more important to advocate for systemic changes.

The stories you read earlier about my grandmother, my mother, and thousands of other women before them are a testament to the power of perseverance in personal finance and the fight for financial independence, first on a personal level and then on a societal scale. Changing this story means getting rid of gender, race, and class biases that keep financial inequality going. Instead, we need to create a future in which young women and girls see financial independence as a celebration and a skill that is taught from the start, not as a battle won against societal obstacles.

## We Are Challenged First, Doubted Second, and Believed Third

Financial independence is how we claim space in an economy that has historically sidelined us. It's how we rewrite the narrative that has been handed down to us through generations and assert ourselves in personal financial conversations that have tried to silence us. That is what The Broke Black Girl was; it's what it still is. It is a revolt, an act of defiance against an economic system that failed me and has continued to fail many Black women like me. It is a response that started from exhaustion and urgency and turned into a space for financial refuge and empowerment.

*Why do spaces like this need to exist in the first place?*

This is a question I still find myself battling with today. Although the answer is obvious to me, it still seems like a difficult concept to grasp for many people outside our circle. Had I explained to someone in my male-dominated field how my son's question about my sandals made me feel emotionally and financially, I would've been written off as dramatic or met with some story about how everyone has their struggles. I would've been told to just work harder, make more money, or manage my money better without understanding the barriers and challenges I am more likely to face as a woman, especially a single Black mother, that led to me only being able to afford the sandals in the first place. This is deeper than a pair of sandals.

Men have dominated and shaped the financial industry by using their perspectives to influence financial education for everyone else. Yet presently, women have positioned themselves to be the breadwinners of their households while leading in education and new business start-ups, all while being paid less. It would make sense that personal finance conversations be shaped in a way that centers women. When women have access to equitable financial resources and spaces, we can create a life for ourselves and those who depend on us that no one else can control. Equitable financial resources have come to women only through our own tireless advocacy—something we've screamed, fought, and even died for. Women have had to fight to get their own bank accounts, own a home without a man, get access to credit, and have the right to work, and even today we are still fighting to get paid equally and fairly.

We see it when we hear dismissive remarks about "women's issues" in finance or when the challenges women face are overlooked or minimized. We see it when the burden of proof disproportionately falls on women to showcase our financial knowledge or justify our financial decisions before we are taken seriously. We see it in the comments of our celebratory social media posts after we've paid off hundreds of thousands of dollars of debt, invested our first $100,000, purchased a new home, obtained a new degree, or doubled our income. Comments masked as "Must be nice" or "Do you have proof of this?" or "So you mean to tell me you didn't already know this?" often undermine our achievements and knowledge and hint at the skepticism and extra scrutiny directed at women when sharing our financial success, knowledge, and challenges. **We are challenged first, doubted second, and believed third.**

We need these safe spaces to exist because they are just that—safe. Safe spaces for women to discuss our experiences with money and the inequalities that have traditionally kept women from achieving financial security. Such spaces offer more than just financial advice; they provide a supportive community where we can not only learn from other women who face similar challenges but also be validated in our experience with money without having to convince anyone of the legitimacy of our financial concerns. How many times have you felt the need or pressure to justify your financial decisions, from your investment choices to your credit card usage or daily expenses, in a way that your male counterparts are rarely required to do? This constant need for justification from society adds a whole layer of emotional stress on women and can deter many from taking a more active role in their finances. This is why safe spaces where women can openly discuss and learn about finance are so important. These environments not only protect women from unwarranted and harmful opinions but also provide a nurturing environment for financial growth and empowerment.

The Broke Black Girl started with one member, my youngest sister, and within a few months, we had over fifty thousand women in our community. When women gather in these communities, they are not just sharing tips on saving, debt, and investing; they are collectively breaking down the barriers that have long made our personal finance journey difficult.

The history of women working together to advance their financial stability and communities shows how powerful these communities, online and offline, can be. From women fighting for women's rights to work, own property, and manage their own finances to present-day networks that connect women with shared interests in finance, entrepreneurship, and real estate, these communities have played a pivotal role in shifting societal views and increasing financial literacy among women. The role of community in these spaces is invaluable. We've seen continuous growth in how women engage with money, from being intimidated and passive with their strategies to becoming active investors, aggressive negotiators, and proactive planners.

But while community support is important, and we've seen what happens when we work together, individual action is equally powerful. I remember how my early days of trying to figure this money thing out left me feeling overwhelmed and uncertain, and before I could seek help from a community of like-minded people or make use of any available resources, I had to take the first step on my own. It required a moment of self-reflection and commitment to change. I needed to be honest with myself and take accountability for my financial situation, no matter how messed up things were.

## Taking Responsibility for Yourself

Taking accountability meant owning up to the fact that I wasn't always budgeting properly. Sure, I may have created the budget at the beginning of the month, but I wasn't *really* tracking my expenses and accounting for *all* the times I swiped my card. I had to admit that my spending habits were a little out of control in some areas and that they were mostly fueled by emotional purchases and the false sense of security they provided. I had to admit that the reason I was a few dollars short on bills at times was not *always* a result of "not making enough money" but *also* because small purchases like vending machines and last-minute cash register purchases added up enough to push me outside my budget, even if just by a few dollars. I had to face the reality that I was procrastinating on some important financial tasks, like paying bills on time and opening my mail to review bank statements on a regular basis.

I had to acknowledge the lies I was telling myself that I would pick up overtime later or spend less next week to make up for overspending now and convincing myself that I needed to "stop at the store and grab something really quick" when I did not. I had to confront my reliance on credit cards and the "Bank of My Momma" and address the root cause of my financial issues beyond my circumstances. This doesn't mean that those outside forces were not real—two things can be true at once—but I had to look at myself in the mirror and realize that fault and responsibility don't always fall on the same shoulders. This means that while most of the challenges I encountered on my personal finance journey were not my fault and contributed to my financial difficulties, I also owed it to myself to take personal responsibility for my financial actions and decisions. True accountability involved me taking owner-ship of the role that I played in my situation, and by doing so, I was able to take control of my finances. Keep in mind that "taking control of my finances" doesn't mean that everything is fixed. It simply means I'm aware of what went wrong and have the knowledge to work toward my desired outcomes. This shift in perspective allowed me to transform my approach to personal finance by using challenges as an opportunity for accountability, advocacy, and achievement.

With this newfound understanding, I want to share some things to consider when leveraging the power of perseverance in personal finance. Throughout this book, we've discussed the small and deliberate actions you can take toward improving your finances, but I want us to take a moment to focus on what you can do to improve your mind:

- **Take time to reflect on your financial journey and the obstacles you've overcome.** Acknowledge your resilience and how that has shaped your financial decisions. This is about understanding your story and using it as motivation to keep going.

- **View financial mistakes as learning opportunities, not failures.** Each mistake you've made was and still is a chance to learn and improve your financial habits and use them to build a stronger foundation.

- **Draw strength from the perseverance and resilience demonstrated by previous generations in your family.** Think about the struggles and triumphs that your parents, grandparents, and great-grandparents faced, and use their stories as inspiration to guide you on your journey.

- **Visualize yourself at your highest.** Create a vision board that represents your financial goals. Include images and quotes that remind you to stay focused and motivated, especially during challenging times.

- **Cultivate a positive mindset.** Use positive affirmations to reinforce your belief in your ability to be financially successful and increase your confidence when it comes to handling money, no matter how difficult it may seem.

- **Never stop learning.** Equip yourself with knowledge by taking advantage of the different resources available, from books and online classes to financial workshops and webinars. But don't stop there; you need to stay up to date on financial news, politics, and more. The more you know, the more confident you'll feel about managing your money.

Remember, many of us were not taught financial literacy, but the power to push forward is something that has been passed down to us from generation to generation.

Your wake-up call may not be a divorce, the loss of a parent, or your child inquiring why you are wearing sandals when it's cold outside. Your wake-up call may be a declined debit card at the grocery store, the stack of unpaid bills on your kitchen counter, or the stress of not having enough money saved to cover a $200 emergency. It could be a conversation you overhear your child having with a friend, realizing they've picked up your bad money habits, or something you've read in this book that you've been struggling to put into words. Whatever it is, that moment of clarity is going to act as a turning point, urging you to confront your financial reality and take responsibility for your financial future.

Just take a look at our history: We've faced more than our share of challenges and we've come through stronger every single time. We are the backbones of our families and communities, holding everyone and everything together. Our resilience is unmatched, and our power to persevere is undeniable. Money should not be another hurdle that holds us back or dims our light. It's time to change that narrative. It's time to reclaim our financial power and build the wealth we deserve. We are owed that. *We owe ourselves that.* When we confront our financial reality head-on, we not only change our own lives but also set a powerful example for other women watching us.

Opening a savings account, paying down debt, investing your first dollar, creating a budget, negotiating your salary—these are all acts of courage and defiance of a system that was created to work against us. These are reminders that we kept going, even when it was hard. We are living testaments to the Black women who came before us, who fought for our right not only to be financially stable but to thrive. We honor their legacy by continuing to push forward, sharing our financial stories with each other, celebrating our wins, showing up authentic and raw, even if that means showing up broke and vulnerable, like I did in 2017, and helping each other out when things get tough. We are stronger together.

To every woman reading this, you are stronger than you realize, capable, and worthy of financial freedom. This freedom is within your reach as it was within mine, and it starts with taking control today. Every small step you take toward financial independence is a victory.

If you've made it this far, you've already taken the first step.

We got this. Let's move beyond broke.

# Acknowledgments

First and foremost, I want to thank God for blessing me with my mom, Shirese; your unwavering support, love, and belief in me have been the foundation upon which I've built my life and this journey. To my late father, John, your memory and teachings have been my guiding light. I carry your strength with me every day.

To my two incredible sons, Camryn and Woo, you are my inspiration and my greatest joy. We've sacrificed so much together over the last year, and your patience, understanding, and love have kept me grounded and motivated.

To my siblings, as your eldest sister, I have always felt a deep responsibility to guide and protect you, but in truth, you have been my biggest teachers. Thank you for being my anchors and for reminding me every day of the power of family. Combined for life!

A special thank-you to my creative team—Christina, Mena, Karen, Jaime, and Pee Kay. Your creativity and dedication helped me present my best self to the world, and I couldn't have done it without you.

To my friends and family, thank you for the grace and love you showed me throughout this process, especially during the times I was distant and slow to respond to messages. Your understanding means more to me than words can express.

To my literary team—Leigh, Maria, and Juliane—thank you for being there with me through every draft, every late night, and every challenge. Your belief in this project and your guidance made this book a reality. To my editor, Stephanie, thank you for seeing value in my work and voice. From discovering just a few short words of mine, you trusted me with an **entire** book. Your faith in my story and your commitment to bringing out the best in my writing have meant the world to me.

To the publishing team, Karina, Francesca, Clare, Stacey, and Richard, your support and expertise have been invaluable. Thank you for believing in this project and for helping shape it into something I'm truly proud of.

To The Broke Black Girl (TBBG) community, you are the heartbeat of my work. Your stories, your strength, and your perseverance continue to inspire me every single day. This book is as much yours as it is mine.

Finally, to my hometown, St. Louis, thank you for first believing in me. Your support has carried me further than I could have ever imagined.

This book is a testament to all of you. Thank you for being part of this journey with me.

# Index

# About the Author

Dasha Kennedy is a financial activist based in Georgia, originally from St. Louis, Missouri, and the creator of the award-winning financial advocacy group The Broke Black Girl. After quickly climbing the ranks in the finance industry, starting at the age of nineteen, Kennedy took a different approach to providing financial literacy to underserved people, primarily women. With over a decade of personal finance education, both formal and informal, Kennedy has shifted the personal finance world with her culturally competent and relevant approach. Women can inhabit a uniquely difficult space in America, confronting financial, social, and racial challenges all at once. In the face of all this, Dasha Kennedy uses her digital community to provide ready-to-use and easy-to-digest financial information to those who have often been overlooked in traditional conversations about personal finance.